50 Southern BBQ Secrets Recipes for Home

By: Kelly Johnson

Table of Contents

- Pulled Pork
- Smoked Brisket
- Baby Back Ribs
- BBQ Chicken
- Texas-style Beef Ribs
- Memphis Dry Rub Ribs
- Carolina Pulled Pork Sandwiches
- Kansas City BBQ Sauce
- Alabama White BBQ Sauce
- South Carolina Mustard BBQ Sauce
- Smoked Sausage
- BBQ Baked Beans
- Cornbread
- Macaroni and Cheese
- Collard Greens
- Brunswick Stew
- BBQ Pulled Chicken Sandwiches
- BBQ Pork Sliders
- BBQ Beef Brisket Sandwiches
- Smoked Turkey Legs
- BBQ Pork Belly Burnt Ends
- BBQ Pork Spare Ribs
- BBQ Chicken Wings
- BBQ Shrimp
- BBQ Meatloaf
- BBQ Chicken Thighs
- BBQ Pork Chops
- BBQ Beef Short Ribs
- BBQ Potato Salad
- BBQ Coleslaw
- BBQ Pork Tacos
- BBQ Chicken Skewers
- BBQ Brisket Nachos
- BBQ Jalapeno Poppers
- BBQ Stuffed Bell Peppers
- BBQ Brisket Chili

- BBQ Bacon Wrapped Shrimp
- BBQ Pulled Pork Pizza
- BBQ Chicken Pizza
- BBQ Beef Brisket Pizza
- BBQ Chicken Salad
- BBQ Pork Sandwiches
- BBQ Beef Sandwiches
- BBQ Beef Ribs
- BBQ Brisket Tacos
- BBQ Pork Belly
- BBQ Chicken Thighs
- BBQ Beef Burgers
- BBQ Smoked Chicken
- BBQ Pulled Pork Egg Rolls

Pulled Pork

Ingredients:

- 4-5 lbs pork shoulder (also known as pork butt), boneless or bone-in
- 2 tablespoons brown sugar
- 1 tablespoon paprika
- 1 tablespoon garlic powder
- 1 tablespoon onion powder
- 1 tablespoon cumin
- 1 tablespoon salt
- 1 teaspoon black pepper
- 1 cup barbecue sauce (plus extra for serving)
- 1/2 cup apple cider vinegar
- 1/2 cup chicken or pork broth

Instructions:

1. **Prepare the Pork:**
    - In a small bowl, mix together the brown sugar, paprika, garlic powder, onion powder, cumin, salt, and black pepper to create a dry rub.
    - Pat the pork shoulder dry with paper towels. Rub the dry rub mixture all over the pork shoulder, covering it evenly.
2. **Slow Cook the Pork:**
    - Place the pork shoulder in a slow cooker or crockpot. Pour the apple cider vinegar and broth around the pork (not directly over it).
    - Cover and cook on low for 8-10 hours or on high for 5-6 hours, until the pork is very tender and easily shreds with a fork.
3. **Shred the Pork:**
    - Once cooked, remove the pork shoulder from the slow cooker and place it on a cutting board or large plate.
    - Use two forks to shred the pork into bite-sized pieces, discarding any large pieces of fat.
4. **Combine with Barbecue Sauce:**
    - In a large bowl, combine the shredded pork with 1 cup of barbecue sauce. Mix well to coat the pork evenly. Adjust the amount of sauce according to your preference.
5. **Serve:**
    - Serve the pulled pork hot on toasted buns or over rice.
    - Optionally, serve with extra barbecue sauce on the side for dipping or drizzling.
6. **Enjoy:**
    - Enjoy your homemade pulled pork as a delicious main dish, perfect for gatherings, potlucks, or a comforting family meal.

This Pulled Pork recipe is versatile and can be adapted to your taste preferences. You can customize the seasoning, adjust the sweetness or spiciness of the barbecue sauce, or experiment with different serving options. It's a classic Southern favorite that is sure to be a hit!

Smoked Brisket

Ingredients:

- 1 whole beef brisket, about 10-12 lbs (preferably USDA Choice or Prime)
- 1/4 cup kosher salt
- 1/4 cup coarse ground black pepper
- 2 tablespoons paprika
- 2 tablespoons brown sugar
- 1 tablespoon garlic powder
- 1 tablespoon onion powder
- 1 tablespoon ground cumin
- 1 tablespoon chili powder
- 1 tablespoon mustard powder
- Wood chips or chunks (hickory, oak, or mesquite), soaked in water for 30 minutes

Instructions:

1. **Prepare the Brisket:**
   - Trim any excess fat from the brisket, leaving about 1/4 inch of fat on the surface. This helps keep the brisket moist during smoking.
   - Pat the brisket dry with paper towels.
2. **Make the Dry Rub:**
   - In a small bowl, mix together the kosher salt, black pepper, paprika, brown sugar, garlic powder, onion powder, cumin, chili powder, and mustard powder to create the dry rub.
3. **Season the Brisket:**
   - Rub the dry rub mixture evenly all over the brisket, covering all sides. Press the rub into the meat to ensure it adheres well.
4. **Prepare the Smoker:**
   - Prepare your smoker according to manufacturer's instructions and bring the temperature to 225-250°F (107-121°C). Use indirect heat for smoking.
5. **Smoke the Brisket:**
   - Place the brisket fat-side up on the smoker rack.
   - Add soaked wood chips or chunks to the smoker box or directly onto the coals for smoke flavor.
   - Close the smoker lid and smoke the brisket, maintaining a steady temperature, for about 1.5 hours per pound of brisket. This typically takes 10-12 hours for a 10-12 lb brisket.
6. **Monitor and Maintain Temperature:**
   - Monitor the smoker temperature regularly using a thermometer to ensure it stays within the desired range.
   - Optionally, spritz the brisket occasionally with a mixture of apple cider vinegar and water (50/50 ratio) to keep it moist.

7. **Check for Doneness:**
   - The brisket is done when it reaches an internal temperature of 195-205°F (90-96°C) and probes tenderly with a thermometer or fork. The meat should have a dark crust (bark) and be very tender.
8. **Rest the Brisket:**
   - Remove the brisket from the smoker and wrap it tightly in foil or butcher paper.
   - Let the brisket rest for at least 1 hour to allow the juices to redistribute and the meat to become more tender.
9. **Slice and Serve:**
   - Slice the brisket against the grain into 1/4 to 1/2 inch thick slices.
   - Serve the smoked brisket slices with your favorite barbecue sauce on the side, or enjoy as is for pure smoky goodness.
10. **Enjoy:**
    - Serve your homemade smoked brisket as the star of a barbecue feast, alongside sides like coleslaw, baked beans, cornbread, and potato salad.

This smoked brisket recipe requires patience but rewards you with tender, flavorful meat that captures the essence of classic Southern barbecue. Adjust the seasoning and smoking time according to your preferences and equipment for the perfect smoked brisket every time.

Baby Back Ribs

Ingredients:

- 2 racks of baby back ribs (about 2-3 lbs each)
- Dry Rub:
    - 1/4 cup brown sugar
    - 2 tablespoons paprika
    - 1 tablespoon salt
    - 1 tablespoon black pepper
    - 1 tablespoon garlic powder
    - 1 tablespoon onion powder
    - 1 teaspoon cayenne pepper (optional, for heat)
- BBQ Sauce (optional, for serving)

Instructions:

1. **Prepare the Ribs:**
    - Remove the membrane from the back of the ribs: Use a butter knife to lift and loosen the membrane, then grab it with a paper towel and peel it off.
2. **Make the Dry Rub:**
    - In a small bowl, combine the brown sugar, paprika, salt, black pepper, garlic powder, onion powder, and cayenne pepper (if using). Mix well to create the dry rub.
3. **Season the Ribs:**
    - Pat the ribs dry with paper towels.
    - Rub the dry rub generously all over both sides of the ribs, pressing it into the meat to adhere.
4. **Prepare the Grill:**
    - Preheat your grill to 225-250°F (107-121°C) for indirect heat cooking. Use wood chips or chunks (hickory, apple, or cherry) for smoke flavor, soaked in water for 30 minutes and placed in a smoker box or wrapped in aluminum foil with holes poked on top.
5. **Cook the Ribs:**
    - Place the ribs on the grill, bone-side down, away from direct heat. Close the lid and smoke for 3-4 hours, maintaining a steady temperature and adding more soaked wood chips or chunks as needed for smoke.
6. **Check for Doneness:**
    - The ribs are done when the meat has pulled back from the ends of the bones and is tender. You can test for doneness by gently twisting a bone; it should move freely in the meat.
7. **Optional: Glaze with BBQ Sauce (if desired):**
    - During the last 30 minutes of cooking, brush the ribs with your favorite BBQ sauce, if using. Allow the sauce to caramelize slightly.

8. **Rest and Serve:**
    - Remove the ribs from the grill and let them rest for 10-15 minutes before slicing.
    - Slice between the bones and serve the baby back ribs hot, with additional BBQ sauce on the side if desired.
9. **Enjoy:**
    - Enjoy these tender and flavorful baby back ribs as the main dish for a BBQ gathering or family meal. Serve with classic sides like coleslaw, cornbread, and baked beans for a complete barbecue feast.

This recipe ensures that your baby back ribs are tender, juicy, and packed with smoky flavor. Adjust the cooking time and seasoning according to your preference for the perfect ribs every time.

BBQ Chicken

Ingredients:

- 4 bone-in, skin-on chicken thighs
- 4 bone-in, skin-on chicken drumsticks
- 1 cup BBQ sauce (your favorite variety)
- 2 tablespoons olive oil
- 1 tablespoon paprika
- 1 tablespoon garlic powder
- 1 tablespoon onion powder
- 1 teaspoon salt
- 1 teaspoon black pepper
- Optional: additional BBQ sauce for serving

Instructions:

1. **Prepare the Chicken:**
   - Pat the chicken thighs and drumsticks dry with paper towels.
   - In a small bowl, mix together olive oil, paprika, garlic powder, onion powder, salt, and black pepper to create a seasoning rub.
2. **Season the Chicken:**
   - Rub the seasoning mixture all over the chicken thighs and drumsticks, ensuring they are evenly coated.
3. **Preheat the Grill:**
   - Preheat your grill to medium-high heat (about 375-400°F or 190-200°C) for direct heat cooking.
4. **Grill the Chicken:**
   - Place the chicken pieces on the grill, skin-side down, and close the lid.
   - Grill for 5-7 minutes on each side, or until the internal temperature reaches 165°F (74°C) and the juices run clear when pierced with a fork.
5. **Apply BBQ Sauce:**
   - During the last few minutes of grilling, brush the chicken with BBQ sauce on both sides, turning and basting occasionally to create a sticky glaze.
6. **Check for Doneness:**
   - Ensure the chicken is fully cooked by checking the internal temperature with a meat thermometer. It should register 165°F (74°C) in the thickest part of the meat, away from the bone.
7. **Rest and Serve:**
   - Remove the BBQ chicken from the grill and let it rest for a few minutes before serving.
   - Serve hot with additional BBQ sauce on the side, if desired.
8. **Enjoy:**

- Enjoy your BBQ chicken thighs and drumsticks as a delicious main dish, perfect for summer grilling or any BBQ occasion. Pair with your favorite sides like coleslaw, cornbread, or grilled vegetables for a complete meal.

This BBQ chicken recipe is simple yet flavorful, allowing the natural smokiness of the grill and the tangy sweetness of BBQ sauce to complement the tender chicken meat. Adjust the seasoning and grilling time based on your grill and personal preferences for the perfect BBQ chicken every time.

Texas-style Beef Ribs

Ingredients:

- 2 racks beef ribs (about 4-5 lbs each), preferably beef short ribs
- Salt and black pepper, to taste
- 2 tablespoons olive oil

For the Dry Rub:

- 1/4 cup brown sugar
- 2 tablespoons paprika
- 1 tablespoon chili powder
- 1 tablespoon garlic powder
- 1 tablespoon onion powder
- 1 tablespoon ground cumin
- 1 tablespoon mustard powder
- 1 tablespoon salt
- 1 tablespoon black pepper

Instructions:

1. **Prepare the Ribs:**
   - Remove the membrane from the back of the ribs: Use a butter knife to lift and loosen the membrane, then grab it with a paper towel and peel it off.
   - Pat the ribs dry with paper towels.
2. **Apply the Dry Rub:**
   - In a small bowl, mix together all the dry rub ingredients: brown sugar, paprika, chili powder, garlic powder, onion powder, cumin, mustard powder, salt, and black pepper.
   - Rub the dry rub mixture generously all over the beef ribs, pressing it into the meat to adhere.
3. **Let the Ribs Rest:**
   - Let the ribs sit at room temperature with the dry rub for at least 30 minutes to allow the flavors to penetrate the meat.
4. **Preheat the Smoker:**
   - Preheat your smoker to 225-250°F (107-121°C) using indirect heat. Use wood chips or chunks (hickory or oak) for smoke flavor, soaked in water for 30 minutes and placed in a smoker box or directly on the coals.
5. **Smoke the Ribs:**
   - Place the seasoned beef ribs directly on the smoker grate, bone-side down.
   - Close the smoker lid and smoke the ribs for about 5-6 hours, or until the internal temperature of the ribs reaches 200-205°F (93-96°C) and the meat is tender and pulls away from the bones.
6. **Rest the Ribs:**

- Remove the smoked beef ribs from the smoker and wrap them tightly in aluminum foil.
- Let the ribs rest for at least 30 minutes to 1 hour to allow the juices to redistribute and the meat to become more tender.

7. **Slice and Serve:**
   - Unwrap the ribs and slice between the bones into individual portions.
   - Serve the Texas-style beef ribs hot, with your favorite barbecue sauce on the side if desired.

8. **Enjoy:**
   - Enjoy these flavorful and tender Texas-style beef ribs as a main dish, paired with classic sides like coleslaw, baked beans, or cornbread for a true barbecue feast.

This recipe captures the essence of Texas barbecue with its robust flavors and tender meat. Adjust the seasoning and smoking time according to your preference and equipment for perfect Texas-style beef ribs every time.

Memphis Dry Rub Ribs

Ingredients:

- 2 racks baby back ribs (about 2-3 lbs each)
- For the Dry Rub:
    - 1/4 cup brown sugar
    - 2 tablespoons paprika
    - 1 tablespoon garlic powder
    - 1 tablespoon onion powder
    - 1 tablespoon chili powder
    - 1 tablespoon ground cumin
    - 1 tablespoon ground mustard
    - 1 tablespoon salt
    - 1 tablespoon black pepper
    - 1 teaspoon cayenne pepper (adjust to taste for spiciness)

Instructions:

1. **Prepare the Ribs:**
    - Remove the membrane from the back of the ribs: Use a butter knife to lift and loosen the membrane, then grab it with a paper towel and peel it off.
    - Pat the ribs dry with paper towels.
2. **Make the Dry Rub:**
    - In a small bowl, combine all the dry rub ingredients: brown sugar, paprika, garlic powder, onion powder, chili powder, cumin, ground mustard, salt, black pepper, and cayenne pepper.
3. **Season the Ribs:**
    - Rub the dry rub mixture generously all over both sides of the ribs, pressing it into the meat to adhere.
4. **Let the Ribs Rest:**
    - Let the seasoned ribs sit at room temperature for about 30 minutes to allow the flavors to penetrate the meat.
5. **Prepare the Grill or Smoker:**
    - Preheat your grill or smoker to 225-250°F (107-121°C) for indirect heat cooking. Use wood chips or chunks (hickory or oak) for smoke flavor, soaked in water for 30 minutes and placed in a smoker box or directly on the coals.
6. **Smoke the Ribs:**
    - Place the seasoned ribs on the grill grate, bone-side down, away from direct heat.
    - Close the lid and smoke the ribs for 4-5 hours, or until the ribs are tender and the meat pulls away from the bones.
7. **Rest and Serve:**

- Remove the smoked ribs from the grill and let them rest for 10-15 minutes before slicing.
- Slice the ribs between the bones into individual portions.

8. **Enjoy:**
   - Serve the Memphis-style dry rub ribs hot, with classic sides like coleslaw, baked beans, or potato salad.
   - Optionally, serve with extra barbecue sauce on the side for dipping or drizzling.

These Memphis Dry Rub Ribs are flavorful and tender, showcasing the essence of Memphis barbecue with their robust dry rub seasoning. Adjust the seasoning and smoking time according to your preference for the perfect Memphis-style ribs at home.

Carolina Pulled Pork Sandwiches

Ingredients:

- 4-5 lbs pork shoulder (also known as pork butt), boneless or bone-in
- Salt and black pepper, to taste
- 1 cup apple cider vinegar
- 1/2 cup yellow mustard
- 1/4 cup ketchup
- 1/4 cup brown sugar
- 2 tablespoons hot sauce (such as Tabasco), optional
- 1 tablespoon Worcestershire sauce
- 1 tablespoon paprika
- 1 tablespoon garlic powder
- 1 tablespoon onion powder
- 1 teaspoon cayenne pepper (adjust to taste)
- Hamburger buns or sandwich rolls, for serving

Instructions:

1. **Prepare the Pork:**
   - Pat the pork shoulder dry with paper towels. Season generously with salt and black pepper.
2. **Make the Carolina BBQ Sauce:**
   - In a medium bowl, whisk together the apple cider vinegar, yellow mustard, ketchup, brown sugar, hot sauce (if using), Worcestershire sauce, paprika, garlic powder, onion powder, and cayenne pepper until well combined. This is your Carolina BBQ sauce.
3. **Slow Cook the Pork:**
   - Place the seasoned pork shoulder in a slow cooker or crockpot. Pour half of the Carolina BBQ sauce over the pork, reserving the other half for serving.
   - Cover and cook on low for 8-10 hours or on high for 5-6 hours, until the pork is very tender and easily shreds with a fork.
4. **Shred the Pork:**
   - Once cooked, remove the pork shoulder from the slow cooker and place it on a cutting board or large plate.
   - Use two forks to shred the pork into bite-sized pieces, discarding any large pieces of fat.
5. **Combine with BBQ Sauce:**
   - Transfer the shredded pork to a large bowl. Pour the remaining Carolina BBQ sauce over the pork and toss to coat evenly. Adjust seasoning to taste.
6. **Assemble the Sandwiches:**
   - Toast the hamburger buns or sandwich rolls, if desired.

- Spoon the Carolina pulled pork onto the bottom halves of the buns. Top with coleslaw (optional) and cover with the top halves of the buns.
7. **Serve:**
    - Serve the Carolina Pulled Pork Sandwiches hot, with extra Carolina BBQ sauce on the side for dipping or drizzling.
8. **Enjoy:**
    - Enjoy these flavorful and tangy Carolina Pulled Pork Sandwiches as a hearty meal, perfect for gatherings or a comforting family dinner.

This recipe captures the essence of Carolina-style barbecue with its vinegar-based sauce and tender pulled pork, making it a favorite among BBQ enthusiasts. Adjust the seasoning and spiciness according to your preference for a personalized taste experience.

Kansas City BBQ Sauce

Ingredients:

- 2 cups ketchup
- 1/2 cup apple cider vinegar
- 1/2 cup brown sugar
- 1/4 cup molasses
- 2 tablespoons Worcestershire sauce
- 1 tablespoon smoked paprika
- 1 tablespoon garlic powder
- 1 tablespoon onion powder
- 1 teaspoon black pepper
- 1/2 teaspoon salt
- 1/2 teaspoon cayenne pepper (optional, for heat)

Instructions:

1. **Combine Ingredients:**
   - In a medium saucepan, combine all the ingredients: ketchup, apple cider vinegar, brown sugar, molasses, Worcestershire sauce, smoked paprika, garlic powder, onion powder, black pepper, salt, and cayenne pepper (if using).
2. **Simmer:**
   - Bring the mixture to a boil over medium-high heat, stirring constantly to prevent burning.
   - Reduce the heat to low and simmer for 20-30 minutes, stirring occasionally, until the sauce thickens and flavors meld together.
3. **Adjust Consistency and Seasoning:**
   - If the sauce is too thick, you can thin it out with a bit of water or additional vinegar.
   - Taste and adjust the seasoning, adding more salt, pepper, or cayenne pepper for spiciness if desired.
4. **Cool and Store:**
   - Remove the saucepan from heat and let the Kansas City BBQ sauce cool to room temperature.
   - Transfer the sauce to a jar or airtight container and refrigerate until ready to use. The flavors will continue to develop as it sits.
5. **Serve:**
   - Use Kansas City BBQ sauce as a marinade, basting sauce, or dipping sauce for your favorite grilled meats, pulled pork, ribs, or chicken.
   - Brush it on during the last few minutes of grilling or smoking to caramelize the sauce and enhance the flavors.
6. **Enjoy:**

- Enjoy the rich and tangy flavors of homemade Kansas City BBQ sauce as a delicious addition to your BBQ repertoire. It's perfect for backyard cookouts, parties, or anytime you crave authentic BBQ flavor.

This recipe yields about 3 cups of Kansas City BBQ sauce. Feel free to adjust the sweetness or tanginess to suit your taste preferences. Homemade BBQ sauce can be stored in the refrigerator for up to 2 weeks or frozen for longer storage.

Alabama White BBQ Sauce

Ingredients:

- 1 cup mayonnaise
- 1/4 cup apple cider vinegar
- 1 tablespoon lemon juice
- 1 tablespoon prepared horseradish
- 1 tablespoon Dijon mustard
- 1 tablespoon Worcestershire sauce
- 1 teaspoon salt
- 1/2 teaspoon black pepper
- 1/2 teaspoon garlic powder
- 1/2 teaspoon onion powder
- 1/2 teaspoon smoked paprika
- 1/4 teaspoon cayenne pepper (optional, for heat)
- 1/4 cup finely chopped fresh parsley (optional, for garnish)

Instructions:

1. **Combine Ingredients:**
   - In a medium bowl, whisk together the mayonnaise, apple cider vinegar, lemon juice, prepared horseradish, Dijon mustard, Worcestershire sauce, salt, black pepper, garlic powder, onion powder, smoked paprika, and cayenne pepper (if using). Mix until smooth and well combined.
2. **Adjust Consistency and Seasoning:**
   - If the sauce is too thick, you can thin it out with a bit of water or additional apple cider vinegar.
   - Taste and adjust the seasoning, adding more salt, pepper, or cayenne pepper for spiciness if desired.
3. **Chill and Serve:**
   - Cover the bowl with plastic wrap or transfer the sauce to an airtight container.
   - Refrigerate the Alabama White BBQ Sauce for at least 1 hour before serving to allow the flavors to meld together.
4. **Garnish and Serve:**
   - Before serving, stir the sauce well. Optionally, garnish with finely chopped fresh parsley for added freshness and color.
5. **Enjoy:**
   - Serve Alabama White BBQ Sauce as a dipping sauce for grilled or smoked chicken, turkey, pork, or seafood.
   - It can also be used as a marinade or dressing for salads and coleslaw, adding a tangy and creamy flavor.

Alabama White BBQ Sauce is a versatile condiment that adds a unique twist to your BBQ dishes with its creamy texture and tangy flavor profile. Adjust the ingredients and seasoning to suit your taste preferences for a personalized Alabama-style experience.

South Carolina Mustard BBQ Sauce

Ingredients:

- 1 cup yellow mustard
- 1/2 cup apple cider vinegar
- 1/4 cup honey
- 1/4 cup brown sugar
- 2 tablespoons Worcestershire sauce
- 1 tablespoon hot sauce (such as Tabasco), optional
- 1 teaspoon garlic powder
- 1 teaspoon onion powder
- 1/2 teaspoon smoked paprika
- 1/2 teaspoon black pepper
- 1/2 teaspoon salt

Instructions:

1. **Combine Ingredients:**
   - In a medium saucepan, whisk together the yellow mustard, apple cider vinegar, honey, brown sugar, Worcestershire sauce, hot sauce (if using), garlic powder, onion powder, smoked paprika, black pepper, and salt.
2. **Simmer:**
   - Bring the mixture to a simmer over medium heat, stirring frequently to dissolve the sugar and combine the flavors.
3. **Simmer and Stir:**
   - Reduce the heat to low and simmer for 10-15 minutes, stirring occasionally, until the sauce has thickened slightly and the flavors have melded together.
4. **Adjust Consistency and Seasoning:**
   - If the sauce is too thick, you can thin it out with a bit of water or additional apple cider vinegar.
   - Taste and adjust the seasoning, adding more salt, pepper, or hot sauce for spiciness if desired.
5. **Cool and Serve:**
   - Remove the saucepan from heat and let the South Carolina Mustard BBQ Sauce cool to room temperature.
   - Transfer the sauce to a jar or airtight container and refrigerate until ready to use. The flavors will continue to develop as it sits.
6. **Serve:**
   - Use South Carolina Mustard BBQ Sauce as a marinade, basting sauce, or dipping sauce for grilled meats, especially pork, chicken, or sausages.
   - Brush it on during the last few minutes of grilling to caramelize the sauce and enhance the flavors.
7. **Enjoy:**

- Enjoy the tangy and sweet flavors of homemade South Carolina Mustard BBQ Sauce as a delicious addition to your BBQ dishes. It's perfect for backyard cookouts, picnics, or any occasion where BBQ flavors shine.

This recipe yields about 1.5 cups of South Carolina Mustard BBQ Sauce. Adjust the sweetness, tanginess, or spiciness according to your preference for a personalized BBQ sauce experience. Homemade BBQ sauce can be stored in the refrigerator for up to 2 weeks or frozen for longer storage.

Smoked Sausage

Ingredients:

- 1 lb smoked sausage (such as kielbasa or Andouille), sliced into 1/2-inch thick rounds
- BBQ sauce or mustard BBQ sauce (optional, for serving)

Instructions:

1. **Prepare the Grill or Smoker:**
   - Preheat your grill or smoker to medium-high heat (about 375-400°F or 190-200°C) for direct heat cooking.
2. **Grill the Sausage:**
   - Place the sliced smoked sausage rounds directly on the grill grates.
   - Grill the sausage for about 4-5 minutes per side, or until they are nicely browned and heated through. You can rotate them halfway through cooking for even grill marks.
3. **Optional: Glaze with BBQ Sauce:**
   - During the last few minutes of grilling, you can brush the smoked sausage rounds with your favorite BBQ sauce or mustard BBQ sauce, if desired. Allow the sauce to caramelize slightly.
4. **Check for Doneness:**
   - Ensure the smoked sausage rounds are heated through and have nice grill marks on both sides.
5. **Serve:**
   - Remove the smoked sausage from the grill and transfer them to a serving platter.
   - Serve hot, optionally with additional BBQ sauce or mustard BBQ sauce on the side for dipping.
6. **Enjoy:**
   - Enjoy the smoky and savory flavors of grilled smoked sausage as a delicious main dish or appetizer. It pairs well with coleslaw, potato salad, or grilled vegetables for a complete meal.

This recipe is versatile and allows you to adjust the cooking time and seasoning according to your preference. Whether you enjoy it as a main dish, slice it up for sandwiches, or serve it as part of a BBQ spread, smoked sausage is sure to be a hit at your next gathering.

BBQ Baked Beans

Ingredients:

- 2 cans (15 oz each) of navy beans or pinto beans, drained and rinsed
- 1/2 lb bacon, diced
- 1 small onion, finely chopped
- 1/2 bell pepper (any color), finely chopped
- 1/2 cup BBQ sauce (your favorite variety)
- 1/4 cup ketchup
- 1/4 cup brown sugar
- 2 tablespoons molasses
- 1 tablespoon Worcestershire sauce
- 1 tablespoon mustard (yellow or Dijon)
- 1 teaspoon garlic powder
- 1/2 teaspoon smoked paprika
- Salt and pepper, to taste

Instructions:

1. **Preheat the Oven:**
   - Preheat your oven to 350°F (175°C).
2. **Cook the Bacon and Vegetables:**
   - In a large oven-safe skillet or Dutch oven, cook the diced bacon over medium heat until crispy.
   - Remove some of the excess bacon fat, leaving about 1-2 tablespoons in the skillet.
   - Add the chopped onion and bell pepper to the skillet with the bacon fat. Cook until softened, about 5 minutes.
3. **Combine Ingredients:**
   - Add the drained and rinsed beans to the skillet with the cooked bacon, onion, and bell pepper.
   - In a bowl, mix together the BBQ sauce, ketchup, brown sugar, molasses, Worcestershire sauce, mustard, garlic powder, and smoked paprika. Stir until well combined.
4. **Bake the Beans:**
   - Pour the BBQ sauce mixture over the beans and stir gently to combine everything evenly.
   - Season with salt and pepper to taste.
5. **Bake in the Oven:**
   - Cover the skillet or Dutch oven with a lid or foil.
   - Transfer to the preheated oven and bake for 45 minutes to 1 hour, or until the beans are bubbly and the sauce has thickened.
6. **Serve:**

- Remove from the oven and let the BBQ Baked Beans cool slightly before serving.
- Garnish with chopped parsley or green onions if desired.

7. **Enjoy:**
    - Serve these flavorful BBQ Baked Beans as a side dish alongside grilled meats, burgers, or sandwiches.
    - They also make a great addition to potlucks, picnics, and BBQ parties.

This recipe can be easily doubled or adjusted based on your preferences. The combination of smoky bacon, tangy BBQ sauce, and sweet molasses makes these BBQ Baked Beans a crowd-pleaser. Adjust the sweetness or spiciness of the beans by adding more or less brown sugar or BBQ sauce according to your taste.

Cornbread

Ingredients:

- 1 cup yellow cornmeal
- 1 cup all-purpose flour
- 1/4 cup granulated sugar (optional, adjust sweetness to taste)
- 1 tablespoon baking powder
- 1/2 teaspoon baking soda
- 1/2 teaspoon salt
- 1 cup buttermilk (or substitute with 1 cup milk mixed with 1 tablespoon vinegar or lemon juice, let sit for 5 minutes)
- 1/2 cup unsalted butter, melted and cooled slightly
- 2 large eggs

Instructions:

1. **Preheat the Oven:**
   - Preheat your oven to 375°F (190°C). Grease a 9-inch square baking dish or a 10-inch cast iron skillet with butter or cooking spray.
2. **Mix Dry Ingredients:**
   - In a large bowl, whisk together the cornmeal, flour, sugar (if using), baking powder, baking soda, and salt until well combined.
3. **Combine Wet Ingredients:**
   - In a separate bowl, whisk together the buttermilk, melted butter, and eggs until smooth.
4. **Combine Wet and Dry Ingredients:**
   - Pour the wet ingredients into the dry ingredients. Stir until just combined and no dry flour remains. Be careful not to overmix, as this can result in tough cornbread.
5. **Bake the Cornbread:**
   - Pour the batter into the prepared baking dish or skillet, spreading it out evenly.
   - Bake for 20-25 minutes, or until the top is golden brown and a toothpick inserted into the center comes out clean.
6. **Cool and Serve:**
   - Remove the cornbread from the oven and let it cool in the pan for about 10 minutes.
   - Slice and serve warm. Optionally, drizzle with honey or serve with butter.
7. **Enjoy:**
   - Enjoy this delicious homemade cornbread as a side dish with BBQ, chili, soups, or stews. It's also great on its own as a snack or breakfast treat.

This recipe yields moist and flavorful cornbread with a slightly crisp crust. Adjust the sweetness by varying the amount of sugar added, or omit it entirely for a more savory cornbread. Serve it fresh out of the oven for the best texture and flavor experience.

Macaroni and Cheese

Ingredients:

- 8 ounces (about 2 cups) elbow macaroni or any pasta shape you prefer
- 4 tablespoons unsalted butter
- 1/4 cup all-purpose flour
- 2 cups whole milk
- 1 cup heavy cream (or substitute with more milk for a lighter version)
- 3 cups shredded cheese (sharp cheddar, Gruyere, or a blend of your favorite cheeses)
- 1/2 teaspoon salt, or more to taste
- 1/4 teaspoon black pepper, or more to taste
- 1/4 teaspoon paprika (optional, for color and flavor)
- 1/4 teaspoon garlic powder (optional, for additional flavor)
- 1/2 cup breadcrumbs (optional, for topping)

Instructions:

1. **Cook the Pasta:**
   - Cook the elbow macaroni according to package instructions in a large pot of salted boiling water until al dente. Drain and set aside.
2. **Make the Cheese Sauce:**
   - In a large saucepan, melt the butter over medium heat.
   - Whisk in the flour and cook for 1-2 minutes until bubbly and golden brown, stirring constantly.
3. **Add Milk and Cream:**
   - Gradually whisk in the milk and heavy cream (if using), ensuring there are no lumps.
   - Cook over medium heat, stirring constantly, until the sauce thickens and begins to simmer, about 5-7 minutes.
4. **Add Cheese:**
   - Reduce the heat to low. Gradually stir in the shredded cheese, a handful at a time, until melted and smooth.
   - Continue stirring until all the cheese has melted and the sauce is creamy and thick.
5. **Season the Sauce:**
   - Stir in the salt, black pepper, paprika (if using), and garlic powder (if using). Adjust seasoning to taste.
6. **Combine Pasta and Cheese Sauce:**
   - Add the cooked macaroni to the cheese sauce, stirring gently to coat evenly.
7. **Optional Breadcrumbs Topping:**
   - If using breadcrumbs, melt 2 tablespoons of butter in a skillet over medium heat. Add the breadcrumbs and cook until golden brown and crispy, stirring frequently.
8. **Bake (Optional):**
   - Preheat your oven to 350°F (175°C).
   - Transfer the macaroni and cheese mixture to a greased baking dish. Sprinkle the toasted breadcrumbs evenly over the top.
   - Bake for 20-25 minutes, or until bubbly and golden brown on top.

9. **Serve:**
    - Remove from the oven and let cool for a few minutes before serving.
    - Serve warm as a main dish or side dish.
10. **Enjoy:**
    - Enjoy this creamy and comforting homemade Macaroni and Cheese with your favorite BBQ dishes or as a standalone meal.

This recipe can be customized with different cheeses or additional ingredients like diced ham, cooked bacon, or vegetables for added flavor and variety. Adjust the thickness of the sauce by adding more milk or cream if needed. It's a versatile dish that's sure to be a hit at any gathering or family meal.

Collard Greens

Ingredients:

- 2 bunches collard greens (about 2 pounds), washed and stems removed
- 4 slices thick-cut bacon, chopped (optional, for flavor)
- 1 large onion, finely chopped
- 3 cloves garlic, minced
- 4 cups chicken or vegetable broth
- 1 tablespoon apple cider vinegar or white vinegar
- 1 tablespoon granulated sugar (optional, to balance bitterness)
- 1 teaspoon salt, or to taste
- 1/2 teaspoon black pepper, or to taste
- 1/4 teaspoon red pepper flakes (optional, for heat)
- Hot sauce (optional, for serving)

Instructions:

1. **Prepare the Collard Greens:**
    - Wash the collard greens thoroughly under cold water. Remove the tough stems and ribs from the leaves, then stack the leaves and slice them into 1-inch strips.
2. **Cook the Bacon (Optional):**
    - In a large pot or Dutch oven, cook the chopped bacon over medium heat until crispy, about 5-7 minutes. Remove the bacon with a slotted spoon and set aside, leaving the bacon fat in the pot.
3. **Saute the Onion and Garlic:**
    - Add the chopped onion to the pot with the bacon fat. Cook for 3-4 minutes, stirring occasionally, until the onion becomes translucent.
    - Add the minced garlic and cook for another 1-2 minutes until fragrant.
4. **Add Collard Greens:**
    - Gradually add the collard greens to the pot, stirring to combine with the onion and garlic. Cook for about 5 minutes, allowing the collard greens to wilt down.
5. **Simmer with Broth:**
    - Pour in the chicken or vegetable broth, ensuring the collard greens are submerged. Bring the mixture to a simmer over medium heat.
6. **Season and Simmer:**
    - Stir in the vinegar, sugar (if using), salt, black pepper, and red pepper flakes (if using).
    - Reduce the heat to low, cover the pot partially with a lid, and let the collard greens simmer for 45 minutes to 1 hour, stirring occasionally, until they are tender and flavorful.
7. **Serve:**
    - Taste and adjust seasoning with more salt, pepper, or vinegar if needed.
    - Serve the collard greens hot, spooning them into a serving bowl. Garnish with the cooked bacon (if using) and serve with hot sauce on the side.
8. **Enjoy:**

- Enjoy these delicious collard greens as a side dish alongside BBQ, fried chicken, cornbread, or any Southern meal. They also make a nutritious and flavorful addition to your table.

This recipe serves 4-6 people as a side dish. Collard greens can be prepared ahead of time and stored in the refrigerator for up to 3 days. Reheat gently on the stove before serving to retain their flavor and texture.

Brunswick Stew

Ingredients:

- 1 lb chicken thighs, bone-in and skin-on (you can also use shredded cooked chicken)
- 1 lb pork shoulder or pork butt, diced into small pieces
- 1/2 lb smoked sausage, sliced into rounds
- 1 onion, finely chopped
- 2 cloves garlic, minced
- 2 cups corn kernels (fresh, frozen, or canned)
- 2 cups lima beans or butter beans (fresh, frozen, or canned)
- 2 cups diced tomatoes (canned or fresh)
- 4 cups chicken broth
- 1 cup BBQ sauce (your favorite variety)
- 1/4 cup ketchup
- 2 tablespoons Worcestershire sauce
- 1 tablespoon hot sauce (optional, adjust to taste)
- 1 teaspoon smoked paprika
- Salt and pepper, to taste
- Chopped parsley or green onions, for garnish (optional)

Instructions:

1. **Brown the Meat:**
   - In a large pot or Dutch oven, heat a tablespoon of oil over medium-high heat. Brown the chicken thighs on both sides until golden brown, about 4-5 minutes per side. Remove and set aside.
   - Brown the diced pork shoulder in the same pot until golden brown, about 5-6 minutes. Remove and set aside.
2. **Saute Vegetables:**
   - In the same pot, add the sliced smoked sausage and cook until lightly browned, about 3-4 minutes. Remove and set aside.
   - Add the chopped onion to the pot and sauté until softened, about 3-4 minutes. Add the minced garlic and cook for another 1-2 minutes until fragrant.
3. **Combine Ingredients:**
   - Return the browned meats (chicken thighs, pork shoulder, and smoked sausage) back to the pot.
   - Add the corn kernels, lima beans (or butter beans), diced tomatoes, chicken broth, BBQ sauce, ketchup, Worcestershire sauce, hot sauce (if using), and smoked paprika. Stir to combine.
4. **Simmer:**
   - Bring the stew to a boil over medium-high heat. Once boiling, reduce the heat to low and let it simmer, uncovered, for 1.5 to 2 hours. Stir occasionally to prevent sticking.
5. **Shred Chicken (if using bone-in thighs):**

- If using bone-in chicken thighs, carefully remove them from the stew, shred the meat using two forks, and discard the bones and skin. Return the shredded chicken meat back to the pot.
6. **Season and Serve:**
    - Taste the stew and adjust seasoning with salt and pepper as needed.
    - Serve Brunswick Stew hot, garnished with chopped parsley or green onions if desired.
7. **Enjoy:**
    - Enjoy this hearty Brunswick Stew as a main dish, accompanied by cornbread or crusty bread. It's a comforting and satisfying meal, perfect for chilly evenings or gatherings with family and friends.

This recipe makes a generous amount of Brunswick Stew, perfect for serving a crowd or for leftovers. It freezes well, so you can store leftovers in an airtight container in the freezer for up to 3 months. Reheat gently on the stove or in the microwave before serving.

BBQ Pulled Chicken Sandwiches

Ingredients:

- 4 boneless, skinless chicken breasts (about 1.5 lbs)
- Salt and pepper, to taste
- 1 cup BBQ sauce (your favorite variety)
- 1/2 cup chicken broth or water
- 1 tablespoon olive oil or vegetable oil
- 4-6 hamburger buns or sandwich rolls
- Coleslaw, optional (for serving)

Instructions:

1. **Prepare the Chicken:**
   - Season the chicken breasts with salt and pepper on both sides.
2. **Cook the Chicken:**
   - In a large skillet or frying pan, heat the olive oil over medium-high heat.
   - Add the chicken breasts and cook for 5-6 minutes on each side, or until they are golden brown and cooked through.
3. **Shred the Chicken:**
   - Remove the chicken breasts from the skillet and transfer them to a cutting board. Use two forks to shred the chicken into bite-sized pieces.
4. **Combine with BBQ Sauce:**
   - Return the shredded chicken to the skillet (or a clean pot) over medium heat.
   - Add the BBQ sauce and chicken broth (or water) to the skillet. Stir to combine and coat the chicken evenly with the sauce.
5. **Simmer:**
   - Bring the mixture to a simmer. Reduce the heat to low and let it simmer gently for about 10-15 minutes, stirring occasionally, to allow the flavors to meld together and the sauce to thicken slightly.
6. **Toast the Buns:**
   - While the chicken is simmering, lightly toast the hamburger buns or sandwich rolls under a broiler or in a toaster oven until golden brown.
7. **Assemble the Sandwiches:**
   - Place a generous amount of the BBQ pulled chicken mixture onto the bottom half of each toasted bun.
   - Optionally, top with coleslaw for added crunch and freshness.
8. **Serve:**
   - Close the sandwiches with the top half of the buns.
   - Serve BBQ Pulled Chicken Sandwiches immediately, accompanied by additional BBQ sauce on the side if desired.
9. **Enjoy:**
   - Enjoy these flavorful BBQ Pulled Chicken Sandwiches as a delicious meal, perfect for lunch, dinner, or any casual gathering.

This recipe is versatile, and you can adjust the seasoning and BBQ sauce according to your taste preferences. Serve these sandwiches with your favorite side dishes like potato salad, coleslaw, or corn on the cob for a complete meal.

BBQ Pork Sliders

Ingredients:

- 2 lbs pork shoulder or pork butt
- Salt and pepper, to taste
- 1 cup BBQ sauce (your favorite variety), plus extra for serving
- 12 slider buns or small dinner rolls
- Coleslaw, for topping (optional)

Instructions:

1. **Prepare the Pork:**
   - Season the pork shoulder or pork butt with salt and pepper on all sides.
2. **Cook the Pork:**
   - Option 1: Slow Cooker Method
     - Place the seasoned pork shoulder or pork butt in a slow cooker.
     - Pour 1 cup of BBQ sauce over the pork, ensuring it's evenly coated.
     - Cook on low for 8 hours or on high for 4-5 hours, until the pork is very tender and easily pulls apart with a fork.
     - Remove the pork from the slow cooker and shred it using two forks. Return the shredded pork to the slow cooker to coat it with the remaining sauce.
   - Option 2: Oven Method
     - Preheat your oven to 300°F (150°C).
     - Place the seasoned pork shoulder or pork butt in a roasting pan or oven-safe dish.
     - Pour 1 cup of BBQ sauce over the pork, ensuring it's evenly coated.
     - Cover tightly with foil and roast in the preheated oven for 4-5 hours, until the pork is tender and pulls apart easily with a fork.
     - Remove from the oven and shred the pork using two forks. Toss the shredded pork in the remaining sauce.
3. **Assemble the Sliders:**
   - Slice the slider buns or dinner rolls in half horizontally.
   - Place a generous amount of BBQ pulled pork on the bottom half of each bun.
   - Top with coleslaw, if desired, for added crunch and freshness.
4. **Serve:**
   - Close the sliders with the top half of the buns.
   - Serve BBQ Pork Sliders immediately, with extra BBQ sauce on the side for dipping or drizzling.
5. **Enjoy:**
   - Enjoy these delicious BBQ Pork Sliders as a crowd-pleasing appetizer or main dish. They're perfect for game day, parties, or any casual gathering.

This recipe can be easily adjusted based on your preferences. Feel free to add additional toppings like pickles, onions, or cheese to customize your sliders. Serve with sides like potato chips, fries, or a simple green salad for a complete meal.

BBQ Beef Brisket Sandwiches

Ingredients:

- 3-4 lbs beef brisket, trimmed of excess fat
- Salt and pepper, to taste
- 1 cup BBQ sauce (your favorite variety), plus extra for serving
- 1 onion, thinly sliced
- 4-6 sandwich buns or rolls, preferably sturdy enough to hold the brisket and sauce
- Coleslaw, for topping (optional)

Instructions:

1. **Prepare the Brisket:**
   - Preheat your oven to 300°F (150°C).
2. **Season and Sear the Brisket:**
   - Season the brisket generously with salt and pepper on all sides.
   - Heat a large oven-safe pot or Dutch oven over medium-high heat. Add a bit of oil and sear the brisket on all sides until browned, about 4-5 minutes per side. Remove the brisket from the pot and set aside.
3. **Cook the Brisket:**
   - In the same pot, add the sliced onions and cook until softened, about 5 minutes.
   - Return the brisket to the pot, placing it on top of the onions.
   - Pour 1 cup of BBQ sauce over the brisket, spreading it evenly to coat.
   - Cover the pot with a lid or tightly with foil.
4. **Slow Roast in the Oven:**
   - Place the covered pot in the preheated oven and roast for 4-5 hours, or until the brisket is tender and easily pulls apart with a fork.
5. **Shred the Brisket:**
   - Remove the pot from the oven and carefully transfer the brisket to a cutting board.
   - Use two forks to shred the brisket into bite-sized pieces. Place the shredded brisket back into the pot with the sauce and onions, stirring to combine and coat evenly.
6. **Assemble the Sandwiches:**
   - Slice the sandwich buns or rolls in half horizontally.
   - Place a generous amount of BBQ shredded brisket onto the bottom half of each bun.
   - Top with coleslaw, if desired, for added texture and flavor.
7. **Serve:**
   - Close the sandwiches with the top half of the buns.
   - Serve BBQ Beef Brisket Sandwiches immediately, with extra BBQ sauce on the side for dipping or drizzling.
8. **Enjoy:**

- Enjoy these delectable BBQ Beef Brisket Sandwiches as a satisfying meal or appetizer. They're ideal for gatherings, parties, or a hearty family dinner.

This recipe allows for flexibility in BBQ sauce choice and can be adjusted to your preferred level of smokiness and sweetness. Serve these sandwiches with classic BBQ sides like potato salad, corn on the cob, or baked beans for a complete BBQ meal experience.

Smoked Turkey Legs

Ingredients:

- 4 turkey legs
- Olive oil or vegetable oil
- Salt and pepper, to taste
- Your favorite dry rub seasoning (optional)
- BBQ sauce (optional, for serving)

Instructions:

1. **Prepare the Turkey Legs:**
   - Rinse the turkey legs under cold water and pat them dry with paper towels.
   - Brush the turkey legs with olive oil or vegetable oil to help the seasoning stick.
2. **Season the Turkey Legs:**
   - Season the turkey legs generously with salt and pepper. Optionally, rub them with your favorite dry rub seasoning for added flavor. Ensure the seasoning covers all sides of the turkey legs evenly.
3. **Prepare the Smoker:**
   - Preheat your smoker to 225-250°F (107-121°C) according to manufacturer's instructions. Use hardwood chips or chunks like hickory, applewood, or cherry for smoking.
4. **Smoke the Turkey Legs:**
   - Place the seasoned turkey legs directly on the smoker rack, making sure there is space between each leg for smoke circulation.
   - Close the smoker and let the turkey legs smoke for 3-4 hours, or until the internal temperature reaches 165°F (74°C) when measured with a meat thermometer inserted into the thickest part of the leg.
5. **Rest and Serve:**
   - Once smoked, remove the turkey legs from the smoker and let them rest for 10-15 minutes before serving. This allows the juices to redistribute.
6. **Optional Serving:**
   - Serve the smoked turkey legs as they are, or brush them with BBQ sauce for a sweet and tangy finish.
7. **Enjoy:**
   - Enjoy these tender and flavorful smoked turkey legs as a main dish. They pair well with coleslaw, cornbread, baked beans, or your favorite BBQ sides.

Smoking turkey legs is a relatively hands-off cooking method that yields delicious results. Adjust the smoking time and temperature based on your smoker's capabilities and desired level of smokiness. This recipe is perfect for outdoor gatherings or any occasion where you want to impress with flavorful and juicy smoked turkey legs.

BBQ Pork Belly Burnt Ends

Ingredients:

- 2 lbs pork belly, skin removed and cut into 1.5-inch cubes
- Your favorite BBQ rub or seasoning
- 1/2 cup BBQ sauce (your choice)
- 1/4 cup honey
- 2 tablespoons unsalted butter
- Salt and pepper, to taste

Instructions:

1. **Prepare the Pork Belly:**
   - Preheat your smoker to 250°F (121°C) using hardwood chips or chunks for smoking. Oak, hickory, or applewood are great options.
2. **Season the Pork Belly:**
   - Place the pork belly cubes in a large bowl. Season them generously with your favorite BBQ rub or seasoning, ensuring all sides are coated evenly.
3. **Smoke the Pork Belly:**
   - Arrange the seasoned pork belly cubes directly on the smoker rack, leaving space between each cube for smoke circulation.
   - Close the smoker and let the pork belly smoke for 2.5-3 hours, or until the cubes have a deep golden-brown color and an internal temperature of about 200°F (93°C).
4. **Make the Glaze:**
   - In a small saucepan over medium heat, combine the BBQ sauce, honey, and butter. Stir until the butter is melted and the glaze is smooth. Season with salt and pepper to taste.
5. **Finish the Burnt Ends:**
   - Remove the smoked pork belly cubes from the smoker and place them in a disposable aluminum pan or baking dish.
   - Pour the BBQ glaze over the pork belly cubes, tossing gently to coat them evenly.
6. **Return to the Smoker:**
   - Place the pan or dish of glazed pork belly cubes back into the smoker.
   - Increase the smoker temperature to 275-300°F (135-149°C) and continue cooking for an additional 1-1.5 hours, or until the pork belly cubes are tender and caramelized.
7. **Rest and Serve:**
   - Remove the BBQ Pork Belly Burnt Ends from the smoker and let them rest for a few minutes.
   - Serve the burnt ends hot as a delicious appetizer or main dish, garnished with chopped parsley or green onions if desired.

8. **Enjoy:**
    - Enjoy these BBQ Pork Belly Burnt Ends with your favorite sides like coleslaw, potato salad, or cornbread for a flavorful and satisfying meal.

BBQ Pork Belly Burnt Ends are a treat for BBQ enthusiasts and a great addition to any backyard cookout or gathering. Adjust the cooking times based on your smoker and desired level of tenderness. The combination of smoky flavors and sweet-savory glaze makes these burnt ends irresistible!

BBQ Pork Spare Ribs

Ingredients:

- 2 racks of pork spare ribs (about 3-4 pounds each)
- Your favorite BBQ rub or seasoning
- 1 cup BBQ sauce (your choice)
- 1/4 cup apple cider vinegar
- 1/4 cup honey or brown sugar
- Salt and pepper, to taste

Instructions:

1. **Prepare the Ribs:**
   - Remove the membrane from the back of the ribs: Use a butter knife to loosen the membrane at one end of the rack, then grip it with a paper towel and peel it off.
2. **Season the Ribs:**
   - Rub the ribs generously with your favorite BBQ rub or seasoning. Make sure to coat both sides evenly.
3. **Preheat and Prepare the Smoker:**
   - Preheat your smoker to 225°F (107°C). Use hardwood chips or chunks like hickory, applewood, or oak for smoking.
4. **Smoke the Ribs:**
   - Place the seasoned ribs on the smoker rack, bone side down. Close the smoker lid.
   - Smoke the ribs for 3-4 hours, maintaining a consistent temperature of 225°F (107°C). You can add more wood chips or chunks throughout the smoking process for additional smoke flavor.
5. **Wrap the Ribs (Optional):**
   - After about 3-4 hours, when the ribs have developed a nice bark (outer crust), you can optionally wrap them in aluminum foil to tenderize them further. This is known as the "Texas crutch."
   - Before wrapping, spritz the ribs with a mixture of apple cider vinegar and water to keep them moist. Optionally, you can add a bit of honey or brown sugar for extra sweetness.
6. **Finish Cooking:**
   - Return the wrapped ribs to the smoker and continue cooking for an additional 1-2 hours, or until the ribs are tender and the meat has pulled back from the bones.
7. **Glaze with BBQ Sauce:**
   - Carefully unwrap the ribs and brush them with BBQ sauce on all sides. Return them to the smoker, unwrapped, for another 15-30 minutes to allow the sauce to set and caramelize slightly.
8. **Rest and Serve:**

- Remove the ribs from the smoker and let them rest for 10-15 minutes before slicing.
- Slice the ribs between the bones and serve immediately with extra BBQ sauce on the side.

9. **Enjoy:**
    - Enjoy these tender and flavorful BBQ Pork Spare Ribs as a main dish, accompanied by classic BBQ sides like coleslaw, baked beans, cornbread, or potato salad.

This recipe ensures tender, juicy ribs with a perfect balance of smoky flavor and sweet-savory BBQ sauce. Adjust the cooking time based on your smoker and desired level of tenderness. BBQ Pork Spare Ribs are sure to be a hit at any BBQ gathering or family meal!

BBQ Chicken Wings

Ingredients:

- 2 lbs chicken wings, drumettes and flats separated
- Salt and pepper, to taste
- Your favorite BBQ rub or seasoning
- 1 cup BBQ sauce (your choice)
- 2 tablespoons unsalted butter, melted
- Optional: chopped fresh parsley or green onions for garnish

Instructions:

1. **Prepare the Chicken Wings:**
    - Preheat your grill to medium-high heat (around 375-400°F / 190-200°C).
2. **Season the Chicken Wings:**
    - Pat the chicken wings dry with paper towels. Season them generously with salt, pepper, and your favorite BBQ rub or seasoning. Ensure all sides of the wings are coated evenly.
3. **Grill the Chicken Wings:**
    - Place the seasoned chicken wings on the preheated grill. Grill them for about 20-25 minutes, turning occasionally, until they are golden brown and cooked through with an internal temperature of 165°F (74°C).
4. **Prepare the BBQ Sauce Glaze:**
    - In a small bowl, mix together the BBQ sauce and melted butter. This creates a flavorful glaze for the wings.
5. **Glaze the Wings:**
    - During the last 5-10 minutes of grilling, start brushing the BBQ sauce glaze onto the chicken wings. Flip the wings and brush the other side as well. Continue to cook until the glaze is caramelized and the wings are nicely coated.
6. **Serve:**
    - Remove the BBQ Chicken Wings from the grill and transfer them to a serving platter.
    - Optionally, sprinkle chopped fresh parsley or green onions over the wings for garnish.
7. **Enjoy:**
    - Serve these delicious BBQ Chicken Wings hot, with extra BBQ sauce on the side for dipping. They're perfect as an appetizer or main dish, paired with celery sticks, carrot sticks, or your favorite dipping sauce.

This recipe is versatile, and you can adjust the seasoning and BBQ sauce according to your taste preferences. Whether you're grilling outdoors or using an indoor grill pan, BBQ Chicken Wings are sure to be a crowd-pleaser!

BBQ Shrimp

Ingredients:

- 1 lb large shrimp, peeled and deveined
- 2 tablespoons olive oil
- Salt and pepper, to taste
- Your favorite BBQ seasoning or dry rub
- 1 cup BBQ sauce (your choice)
- 2 tablespoons unsalted butter, melted
- Optional: chopped fresh parsley or green onions for garnish

Instructions:

1. **Prepare the Shrimp:**
   - Preheat your grill to medium-high heat.
2. **Season the Shrimp:**
   - In a bowl, toss the peeled and deveined shrimp with olive oil, salt, pepper, and your favorite BBQ seasoning or dry rub. Ensure the shrimp are evenly coated with the seasoning.
3. **Skewer the Shrimp (optional):**
   - Thread the seasoned shrimp onto skewers, ensuring they are evenly spaced.
4. **Grill the Shrimp:**
   - Place the shrimp skewers directly on the preheated grill. Grill them for 2-3 minutes per side, or until they are opaque and cooked through. Be careful not to overcook the shrimp, as they can become rubbery.
5. **Prepare the BBQ Sauce Glaze:**
   - In a small bowl, mix together the BBQ sauce and melted butter. This creates a flavorful glaze for the shrimp.
6. **Glaze the Shrimp:**
   - During the last minute of grilling, start brushing the BBQ sauce glaze onto the shrimp skewers. Flip the skewers and brush the other side as well. Continue to cook for another minute or until the sauce is caramelized and the shrimp are nicely coated.
7. **Serve:**
   - Remove the BBQ Shrimp skewers from the grill and transfer them to a serving platter.
   - Optionally, sprinkle chopped fresh parsley or green onions over the shrimp for garnish.
8. **Enjoy:**
   - Serve these delicious BBQ Shrimp skewers hot, with extra BBQ sauce on the side for dipping. They make a fantastic appetizer or main dish, paired with rice, salad, or grilled vegetables.

This recipe is straightforward and allows you to enjoy the natural sweetness of the shrimp complemented by the tangy BBQ sauce. Adjust the seasoning and BBQ sauce according to your taste preferences, and enjoy grilling these BBQ Shrimp for your next outdoor gathering or family meal!

BBQ Meatloaf

Ingredients:

- 1 lb ground beef (or a mix of beef and pork)
- 1 small onion, finely chopped
- 1/2 cup breadcrumbs
- 1/4 cup milk
- 1 egg, lightly beaten
- 2 cloves garlic, minced
- 1/4 cup BBQ sauce (plus extra for topping)
- 1 tablespoon Worcestershire sauce
- 1 teaspoon dried oregano
- 1 teaspoon dried thyme
- Salt and pepper, to taste

For the Glaze:

- 1/2 cup BBQ sauce
- 2 tablespoons brown sugar
- 1 tablespoon apple cider vinegar

Instructions:

1. **Preheat Oven:**
   - Preheat your oven to 350°F (175°C). Grease a loaf pan or line it with parchment paper for easy cleanup.
2. **Prepare the Meatloaf Mixture:**
   - In a large bowl, combine the ground beef, chopped onion, breadcrumbs, milk, beaten egg, minced garlic, 1/4 cup BBQ sauce, Worcestershire sauce, dried oregano, dried thyme, salt, and pepper. Mix until well combined, but avoid overmixing which can make the meatloaf dense.
3. **Shape and Bake the Meatloaf:**
   - Transfer the meatloaf mixture into the prepared loaf pan, shaping it into a loaf shape. Smooth the top with the back of a spoon.
   - Bake in the preheated oven for 45 minutes.
4. **Make the Glaze:**
   - While the meatloaf is baking, prepare the glaze. In a small bowl, mix together 1/2 cup BBQ sauce, brown sugar, and apple cider vinegar until well combined.
5. **Glaze and Finish Baking:**
   - After 45 minutes of baking, remove the meatloaf from the oven. Carefully pour or brush the BBQ glaze over the top of the meatloaf.
   - Return the meatloaf to the oven and bake for an additional 15-20 minutes, or until the internal temperature reaches 160°F (71°C) and the glaze is caramelized.

6. **Rest and Serve:**
   - Remove the meatloaf from the oven and let it rest for 5-10 minutes before slicing.
   - Slice the BBQ Meatloaf and serve hot, drizzling any remaining BBQ sauce from the pan over each slice.
7. **Enjoy:**
   - Serve this BBQ Meatloaf with mashed potatoes, roasted vegetables, or your favorite sides. It's a comforting and satisfying dish that's perfect for family dinners or gatherings.

This recipe allows you to enjoy the classic flavors of meatloaf with a delicious BBQ twist. The glaze adds a sweet and tangy finish that complements the savory meatloaf perfectly. Adjust the seasonings and BBQ sauce according to your taste preferences, and enjoy this hearty dish!

BBQ Chicken Thighs

Ingredients:

- 8 bone-in, skin-on chicken thighs
- Salt and pepper, to taste
- Your favorite BBQ rub or seasoning
- 1 cup BBQ sauce (your choice)
- Optional: chopped fresh parsley or green onions for garnish

Instructions:

1. **Prepare the Chicken Thighs:**
   - Preheat your grill to medium-high heat, around 375-400°F (190-200°C).
2. **Season the Chicken Thighs:**
   - Pat the chicken thighs dry with paper towels. Season them generously with salt, pepper, and your favorite BBQ rub or seasoning. Ensure all sides of the thighs are coated evenly.
3. **Grill the Chicken Thighs:**
   - Place the seasoned chicken thighs skin-side down on the preheated grill. Close the grill lid.
   - Grill the chicken thighs for 6-7 minutes per side, or until the skin is crispy and golden brown, and the internal temperature reaches 165°F (74°C).
4. **Glaze with BBQ Sauce:**
   - During the last few minutes of grilling, start brushing the BBQ sauce onto the chicken thighs. Flip the thighs and brush the other side as well. Continue grilling for another 1-2 minutes per side, allowing the sauce to caramelize slightly.
5. **Check for Doneness:**
   - Use a meat thermometer to ensure the chicken thighs reach an internal temperature of 165°F (74°C) in the thickest part of the meat, without touching the bone.
6. **Serve:**
   - Remove the BBQ Chicken Thighs from the grill and transfer them to a serving platter.
   - Optionally, sprinkle chopped fresh parsley or green onions over the chicken thighs for garnish.
7. **Enjoy:**
   - Serve these delicious BBQ Chicken Thighs hot, with extra BBQ sauce on the side for dipping. They pair well with coleslaw, corn on the cob, baked beans, or your favorite BBQ sides.

This recipe is straightforward and allows you to enjoy tender and flavorful BBQ Chicken Thighs with minimal effort. Adjust the seasoning and BBQ sauce according to your taste preferences, and enjoy grilling these chicken thighs for your next outdoor gathering or family meal!

BBQ Pork Chops

Ingredients:

- 4 bone-in pork chops, about 1-inch thick
- Salt and pepper, to taste
- Your favorite BBQ rub or seasoning
- 1 cup BBQ sauce (your choice)
- Optional: chopped fresh parsley or green onions for garnish

Instructions:

1. **Prepare the Pork Chops:**
    - Preheat your grill to medium-high heat, or your oven to 400°F (200°C).
2. **Season the Pork Chops:**
    - Pat the pork chops dry with paper towels. Season them generously with salt, pepper, and your favorite BBQ rub or seasoning. Ensure both sides of the pork chops are evenly coated.
3. **Grill or Bake the Pork Chops:**
    - **Grilling Method:**
        - Place the seasoned pork chops on the preheated grill. Close the grill lid.
        - Grill the pork chops for 4-5 minutes per side, depending on thickness, or until they reach an internal temperature of 145°F (63°C) for medium-rare or 160°F (71°C) for medium, measured with a meat thermometer inserted into the thickest part of the chop.
    - **Baking Method:**
        - Place the seasoned pork chops on a baking sheet lined with parchment paper or aluminum foil.
        - Bake in the preheated oven for 20-25 minutes, or until they reach an internal temperature of 145°F (63°C) for medium-rare or 160°F (71°C) for medium.
4. **Glaze with BBQ Sauce:**
    - During the last few minutes of grilling or baking, start brushing the BBQ sauce onto the pork chops. Flip the chops and brush the other side as well. Continue grilling or baking for another 1-2 minutes per side, allowing the sauce to caramelize slightly.
5. **Check for Doneness:**
    - Use a meat thermometer to ensure the pork chops reach the desired internal temperature without touching the bone.
6. **Rest and Serve:**
    - Remove the BBQ Pork Chops from the grill or oven and let them rest for 5 minutes before serving.
    - Optionally, sprinkle chopped fresh parsley or green onions over the pork chops for garnish.

7. **Enjoy:**
    - Serve these delicious BBQ Pork Chops hot, with extra BBQ sauce on the side for dipping. They pair well with mashed potatoes, grilled vegetables, or a fresh salad.

This recipe is versatile and allows you to enjoy tender and flavorful BBQ Pork Chops with minimal effort. Adjust the seasoning and BBQ sauce according to your taste preferences, and enjoy cooking these pork chops for a quick and satisfying meal!

BBQ Beef Short Ribs

Ingredients:

- 4 lbs beef short ribs, bone-in
- Salt and pepper, to taste
- Your favorite BBQ rub or seasoning
- 1 cup BBQ sauce (your choice)
- Optional: chopped fresh parsley or green onions for garnish

Instructions:

1. **Prepare the Beef Short Ribs:**
   - Preheat your grill to medium-high heat, or preheat your oven to 300°F (150°C) for a low and slow cook.
2. **Season the Short Ribs:**
   - Pat the beef short ribs dry with paper towels. Season them generously with salt, pepper, and your favorite BBQ rub or seasoning. Ensure all sides of the ribs are evenly coated.
3. **Grill or Bake the Short Ribs:**
   - **Grilling Method:**
     - Place the seasoned beef short ribs on the preheated grill. Close the grill lid.
     - Grill the short ribs for about 3-4 minutes per side, or until they develop a nice sear and grill marks.
   - **Baking Method:**
     - Place the seasoned beef short ribs in a baking dish or roasting pan.
     - Cover the dish tightly with aluminum foil.
     - Bake in the preheated oven for 3-4 hours, or until the meat is tender and easily pulls away from the bone.
4. **Glaze with BBQ Sauce:**
   - During the last 30 minutes of cooking (for both grilling and baking methods), start brushing the BBQ sauce onto the beef short ribs. Flip the ribs and brush the other side as well. This allows the sauce to caramelize slightly.
5. **Check for Doneness:**
   - Use a meat thermometer to ensure the beef short ribs reach an internal temperature of about 200°F (93°C) for tender, fall-off-the-bone meat.
6. **Rest and Serve:**
   - Remove the BBQ Beef Short Ribs from the grill or oven and let them rest for 10-15 minutes before serving.
   - Optionally, sprinkle chopped fresh parsley or green onions over the ribs for garnish.
7. **Enjoy:**

- - Serve these delicious BBQ Beef Short Ribs hot, with extra BBQ sauce on the side for dipping. They pair well with coleslaw, roasted potatoes, or cornbread.

This recipe ensures tender and flavorful BBQ Beef Short Ribs with minimal effort. Adjust the seasoning and BBQ sauce according to your taste preferences, and enjoy cooking these ribs for a memorable meal with friends and family!

BBQ Potato Salad

Ingredients:

- 2 lbs potatoes (preferably red or Yukon gold), peeled and cubed
- Salt, to taste
- 1/2 cup mayonnaise
- 1/4 cup BBQ sauce (your choice)
- 1 tablespoon Dijon mustard
- 1/4 cup diced red onion
- 1/4 cup diced celery
- 1/4 cup diced dill pickles
- 2 tablespoons chopped fresh parsley or chives (optional)
- Salt and pepper, to taste
- Paprika, for garnish

Instructions:

1. **Boil the Potatoes:**
   - Place the cubed potatoes in a large pot and cover with cold water. Add a pinch of salt.
   - Bring the water to a boil over medium-high heat, then reduce the heat and simmer for 10-15 minutes, or until the potatoes are tender when pierced with a fork.
2. **Prepare the Dressing:**
   - In a small bowl, whisk together the mayonnaise, BBQ sauce, and Dijon mustard until well combined. Adjust the amount of BBQ sauce to your taste preferences for more or less tanginess.
3. **Assemble the Salad:**
   - Drain the cooked potatoes and let them cool slightly.
   - In a large mixing bowl, combine the cooled potatoes, diced red onion, diced celery, and diced dill pickles.
   - Pour the BBQ dressing over the potato mixture and gently toss until everything is evenly coated.
   - Season with salt and pepper to taste.
4. **Chill and Serve:**
   - Cover the BBQ Potato Salad and refrigerate for at least 1 hour to allow the flavors to meld together.
5. **Garnish and Serve:**
   - Before serving, garnish the BBQ Potato Salad with chopped fresh parsley or chives, and a sprinkle of paprika for color.
6. **Enjoy:**
   - Serve this delicious BBQ Potato Salad chilled as a side dish at BBQs, picnics, or alongside grilled meats. It's a flavorful twist on a classic favorite!

This BBQ Potato Salad recipe is versatile, and you can customize it by adding additional ingredients like bacon, hard-boiled eggs, or different types of pickles. Adjust the seasoning and BBQ sauce according to your taste preferences, and enjoy this tasty side dish with friends and family!

BBQ Coleslaw

Ingredients:

- 4 cups shredded cabbage (green or a mix of green and red cabbage)
- 1 cup shredded carrots
- 1/2 cup mayonnaise
- 1/4 cup BBQ sauce (your choice)
- 1 tablespoon apple cider vinegar
- 1 tablespoon honey or granulated sugar
- 1/2 teaspoon Dijon mustard
- Salt and pepper, to taste
- Optional: chopped fresh parsley or green onions for garnish

Instructions:

1. **Prepare the Dressing:**
   - In a small bowl, whisk together the mayonnaise, BBQ sauce, apple cider vinegar, honey (or sugar), Dijon mustard, salt, and pepper until smooth and well combined. Adjust the sweetness and tanginess by adding more honey or vinegar, according to your taste.
2. **Mix the Coleslaw:**
   - In a large mixing bowl, combine the shredded cabbage and shredded carrots.
3. **Combine with Dressing:**
   - Pour the BBQ dressing over the cabbage and carrots. Gently toss until the vegetables are evenly coated with the dressing.
4. **Chill and Serve:**
   - Cover the BBQ Coleslaw and refrigerate for at least 30 minutes to allow the flavors to meld together. This step helps the coleslaw to develop its best flavor.
5. **Garnish and Serve:**
   - Before serving, garnish the BBQ Coleslaw with chopped fresh parsley or green onions for added freshness and color.
6. **Enjoy:**
   - Serve this delicious BBQ Coleslaw chilled as a side dish with BBQ chicken, ribs, pulled pork sandwiches, or any grilled meats. It's a refreshing and tangy complement to any BBQ meal!

This recipe is easy to customize by adding additional ingredients like chopped bell peppers, red onion, or even pineapple for a sweet twist. Adjust the BBQ sauce and other seasonings to suit your preferences, and enjoy this flavorful BBQ Coleslaw at your next cookout or gathering!

BBQ Pork Tacos

Ingredients:

- 1 lb pork shoulder or pork tenderloin
- Salt and pepper, to taste
- Your favorite BBQ rub or seasoning
- 1 cup BBQ sauce (your choice)
- 8-10 small corn or flour tortillas
- 1 cup shredded lettuce or cabbage
- 1/2 cup diced tomatoes
- 1/4 cup diced red onion
- 1/4 cup chopped fresh cilantro
- Lime wedges, for serving
- Optional toppings: sliced avocado, sour cream, shredded cheese

Instructions:

1. **Prepare the BBQ Pork:**
    - Season the pork shoulder or tenderloin with salt, pepper, and your favorite BBQ rub or seasoning. Ensure all sides of the pork are evenly coated.
2. **Cook the Pork:**
    - **Grilling Method:**
        - Preheat your grill to medium-high heat.
        - Grill the pork for about 15-20 minutes per side, or until the internal temperature reaches 145°F (63°C) for medium-rare or 160°F (71°C) for medium. During the last few minutes of grilling, brush the pork with BBQ sauce, flipping and brushing the other side as well. Allow the sauce to caramelize slightly.
    - **Oven Method:**
        - Preheat your oven to 350°F (175°C).
        - Place the seasoned pork in a baking dish and cover with foil.
        - Bake for 1.5 to 2 hours, or until the pork is tender and easily shreds with a fork. During the last 30 minutes of baking, uncover the pork and brush with BBQ sauce, allowing it to bake uncovered until the sauce caramelizes.
3. **Shred the Pork:**
    - Once cooked, shred the pork using two forks or your fingers.
4. **Assemble the Tacos:**
    - Warm the tortillas in a dry skillet or microwave until soft and pliable.
    - Fill each tortilla with shredded BBQ pork.
    - Top with shredded lettuce or cabbage, diced tomatoes, diced red onion, and chopped fresh cilantro.
5. **Serve:**

- Serve the BBQ Pork Tacos with lime wedges on the side for squeezing over the tacos.
- Optionally, add sliced avocado, sour cream, or shredded cheese as desired.
6. **Enjoy:**
    - These BBQ Pork Tacos are perfect for a delicious and satisfying meal. Serve them as a main course for a casual dinner or at gatherings with friends and family. The smoky BBQ pork paired with fresh taco toppings makes for a flavorful combination that everyone will love!

Feel free to adjust the toppings and seasonings according to your taste preferences. These BBQ Pork Tacos are versatile and can be customized with your favorite taco fillings for a delicious twist on traditional tacos.

BBQ Chicken Skewers

Ingredients:

- 1 lb boneless, skinless chicken breasts or thighs, cut into 1-inch cubes
- Salt and pepper, to taste
- Your favorite BBQ sauce
- Wooden or metal skewers

Instructions:

1. **Prepare the Chicken:**
    - If using wooden skewers, soak them in water for at least 30 minutes to prevent burning on the grill.
2. **Season and Skewer the Chicken:**
    - Season the chicken cubes with salt and pepper.
    - Thread the seasoned chicken onto the skewers, evenly distributing the pieces. Leave a little space between each piece to ensure even cooking.
3. **Grill the Chicken Skewers:**
    - Preheat your grill to medium-high heat.
    - Place the chicken skewers on the grill. Close the lid and grill for about 4-5 minutes per side, or until the chicken is cooked through and has nice grill marks.
4. **Brush with BBQ Sauce:**
    - During the last few minutes of grilling, start brushing the BBQ sauce onto the chicken skewers. Flip the skewers and brush the other side as well. Allow the sauce to caramelize slightly.
5. **Check for Doneness:**
    - Use a meat thermometer to ensure the chicken reaches an internal temperature of 165°F (74°C).
6. **Serve:**
    - Remove the BBQ Chicken Skewers from the grill and transfer them to a serving platter.
    - Optionally, brush additional BBQ sauce over the skewers before serving for extra flavor.
7. **Enjoy:**
    - Serve these delicious BBQ Chicken Skewers hot, with extra BBQ sauce on the side for dipping. They make a fantastic main dish or appetizer for BBQs, parties, or weeknight dinners.

This recipe is versatile, and you can adjust the seasoning and BBQ sauce according to your taste preferences. BBQ Chicken Skewers are a crowd-pleaser and a great addition to any grilling menu!

BBQ Brisket Nachos

Ingredients:

- 1 lb cooked BBQ brisket, shredded or chopped
- 1 bag (about 10-12 oz) tortilla chips
- 2 cups shredded cheese (cheddar, Monterey Jack, or a blend)
- 1/2 cup BBQ sauce (your favorite)
- 1/2 cup diced red onion
- 1/2 cup diced tomatoes
- 1/4 cup sliced jalapeños (optional)
- 1/4 cup chopped fresh cilantro
- Sour cream and guacamole, for serving

Instructions:

1. **Prepare the BBQ Brisket:**
   - Ensure the BBQ brisket is cooked and shredded or chopped into bite-sized pieces. You can use leftover BBQ brisket or cook it specifically for this recipe.
2. **Preheat the Oven:**
   - Preheat your oven to 400°F (200°C).
3. **Assemble the Nachos:**
   - Spread a layer of tortilla chips evenly on a large baking sheet or oven-safe dish.
   - Sprinkle half of the shredded cheese over the chips.
   - Distribute the cooked BBQ brisket evenly over the cheese layer.
   - Drizzle half of the BBQ sauce over the brisket.
4. **Add More Layers:**
   - Add another layer of tortilla chips on top of the brisket layer.
   - Sprinkle the remaining shredded cheese over the chips.
   - Scatter diced red onion, diced tomatoes, and sliced jalapeños (if using) over the cheese.
5. **Bake the Nachos:**
   - Place the baking sheet or dish in the preheated oven and bake for about 10-12 minutes, or until the cheese is melted and bubbly.
6. **Garnish and Serve:**
   - Remove the BBQ Brisket Nachos from the oven.
   - Drizzle the remaining BBQ sauce over the nachos.
   - Garnish with chopped fresh cilantro.
7. **Serve:**
   - Serve the BBQ Brisket Nachos hot, with sour cream and guacamole on the side if desired.
8. **Enjoy:**

- These BBQ Brisket Nachos are perfect for sharing as an appetizer or enjoying as a main dish. They're great for parties, game days, or any casual gathering where you want to impress with delicious, flavorful nachos!

Feel free to customize these nachos by adding more toppings like black beans, corn kernels, or additional cheese. Adjust the amount of BBQ sauce according to your taste preferences for a perfect balance of flavors.

BBQ Jalapeno Poppers

Ingredients:

- 12 fresh jalapeño peppers
- 8 oz cream cheese, softened
- 1 cup shredded cheddar cheese (or your favorite melting cheese)
- 1/2 teaspoon garlic powder
- 1/2 teaspoon onion powder
- Salt and pepper, to taste
- 12 slices of bacon, cut in half crosswise
- BBQ sauce (your favorite), for brushing
- Toothpicks or skewers, for securing

Instructions:

1. **Prepare the Jalapeños:**
   - Preheat your grill to medium-high heat, or preheat your oven to 400°F (200°C).
2. **Prepare the Filling:**
   - In a mixing bowl, combine the softened cream cheese, shredded cheddar cheese, garlic powder, onion powder, salt, and pepper. Mix until well combined and smooth.
3. **Stuff the Jalapeños:**
   - Cut each jalapeño in half lengthwise and remove the seeds and membranes (use gloves to protect your hands if sensitive to jalapeños).
   - Fill each jalapeño half with the cheese mixture, packing it in slightly.
4. **Wrap with Bacon:**
   - Wrap each stuffed jalapeño half with a half-slice of bacon, securing it with a toothpick or skewer.
5. **Grill or Bake the Poppers:**
   - **Grilling Method:**
     - Place the bacon-wrapped jalapeño poppers on the preheated grill. Close the lid and grill for about 10-12 minutes, turning occasionally, or until the bacon is crispy and the jalapeños are tender.
   - **Oven Method:**
     - Place the bacon-wrapped jalapeño poppers on a baking sheet lined with parchment paper or aluminum foil.
     - Bake in the preheated oven for 20-25 minutes, or until the bacon is crispy and the jalapeños are tender.
6. **Brush with BBQ Sauce:**
   - During the last few minutes of grilling or baking, brush the BBQ sauce over the bacon-wrapped jalapeño poppers. Flip them and brush the other side as well. Allow the sauce to caramelize slightly.
7. **Serve:**

- - Remove the BBQ Jalapeño Poppers from the grill or oven.
  - Serve them hot as a delicious appetizer or snack.
8. **Enjoy:**
   - These BBQ Jalapeño Poppers are spicy, creamy, and savory with a touch of BBQ sweetness. They're perfect for parties, game days, or any gathering where you want to spice things up!

Feel free to adjust the filling by adding cooked and crumbled sausage, chopped herbs, or other cheeses for variation. These poppers are versatile and can be customized to suit your taste preferences for a delightful and flavorful treat.

BBQ Stuffed Bell Peppers

Ingredients:

- 4 large bell peppers (any color), tops cut off and seeds removed
- 1 lb ground beef or turkey
- 1 small onion, diced
- 2 cloves garlic, minced
- 1 cup cooked rice (white or brown)
- 1 cup BBQ sauce (your favorite)
- 1 cup shredded cheddar cheese (or your favorite cheese)
- Salt and pepper, to taste
- Optional: chopped fresh parsley or green onions for garnish

Instructions:

1. **Prepare the Bell Peppers:**
   - Preheat your oven to 375°F (190°C).
2. **Cook the Filling:**
   - In a large skillet, cook the ground beef or turkey over medium heat until browned and cooked through, breaking it up with a spoon as it cooks.
   - Add the diced onion and minced garlic to the skillet. Cook for another 3-4 minutes until the onion is softened.
3. **Combine with Rice and BBQ Sauce:**
   - Stir in the cooked rice and 3/4 cup of BBQ sauce into the skillet with the meat mixture. Season with salt and pepper to taste. Cook for another 2-3 minutes, stirring occasionally, until everything is heated through and well combined.
4. **Stuff the Bell Peppers:**
   - Place the hollowed-out bell peppers upright in a baking dish.
   - Spoon the BBQ meat and rice mixture evenly into each bell pepper, pressing it down gently to pack it in.
5. **Bake the Stuffed Bell Peppers:**
   - Drizzle the remaining 1/4 cup of BBQ sauce over the stuffed bell peppers.
   - Cover the baking dish with aluminum foil and bake in the preheated oven for 30-35 minutes, or until the bell peppers are tender.
6. **Add Cheese and Bake Again:**
   - Remove the foil from the baking dish. Sprinkle the shredded cheddar cheese evenly over the tops of the stuffed bell peppers.
   - Return the dish to the oven and bake, uncovered, for another 10 minutes, or until the cheese is melted and bubbly.
7. **Garnish and Serve:**
   - Remove the BBQ Stuffed Bell Peppers from the oven and let them cool slightly.
   - Garnish with chopped fresh parsley or green onions if desired.
8. **Enjoy:**

- Serve these delicious BBQ Stuffed Bell Peppers hot as a main dish. They are hearty, flavorful, and a perfect way to enjoy BBQ flavors in a comforting and satisfying meal!

These BBQ Stuffed Bell Peppers are versatile, and you can customize the filling by adding beans, corn, or different types of cheese. Adjust the BBQ sauce according to your taste preferences for a perfect balance of flavors.

BBQ Brisket Chili

Ingredients:

- 1 lb cooked BBQ brisket, chopped or shredded
- 1 tablespoon olive oil
- 1 onion, diced
- 3 cloves garlic, minced
- 1 red bell pepper, diced
- 1 green bell pepper, diced
- 2 jalapeño peppers, seeded and finely diced (optional, for heat)
- 1 can (15 oz) black beans, drained and rinsed
- 1 can (15 oz) kidney beans, drained and rinsed
- 1 can (15 oz) diced tomatoes
- 1 cup beef broth
- 1/2 cup BBQ sauce (your favorite)
- 2 tablespoons tomato paste
- 2 teaspoons chili powder
- 1 teaspoon ground cumin
- 1/2 teaspoon smoked paprika
- Salt and pepper, to taste
- Optional toppings: shredded cheese, sour cream, chopped cilantro, diced avocado

Instructions:

1. **Prepare the Brisket:**
   - Ensure the BBQ brisket is cooked and chopped or shredded into bite-sized pieces. You can use leftover BBQ brisket or cook it specifically for this recipe.
2. **Saute the Vegetables:**
   - In a large pot or Dutch oven, heat olive oil over medium heat. Add diced onion and cook for 3-4 minutes until softened.
   - Add minced garlic, diced red bell pepper, green bell pepper, and jalapeño peppers (if using). Cook for another 3-4 minutes until the peppers are tender.
3. **Combine Ingredients:**
   - Add the chopped or shredded BBQ brisket to the pot with the sautéed vegetables.
   - Stir in the black beans, kidney beans, diced tomatoes (with juices), beef broth, BBQ sauce, tomato paste, chili powder, ground cumin, and smoked paprika. Mix well to combine all ingredients.
4. **Simmer the Chili:**
   - Bring the mixture to a simmer over medium-high heat. Reduce the heat to low, cover the pot, and let the chili simmer for 30-40 minutes, stirring occasionally.
5. **Adjust Seasonings:**

- Taste the chili and season with salt and pepper as needed, adjusting the spice level and sweetness with more BBQ sauce or chili powder if desired.
6. **Serve:**
    - Ladle the BBQ Brisket Chili into bowls.
    - Garnish with shredded cheese, a dollop of sour cream, chopped cilantro, and diced avocado if desired.
7. **Enjoy:**
    - Serve this hearty BBQ Brisket Chili hot, with your favorite toppings and crusty bread or cornbread on the side. It's a comforting and flavorful dish that's perfect for cold days or gatherings with friends and family!

This BBQ Brisket Chili recipe is versatile and can be adjusted to suit your taste preferences. Feel free to add more vegetables like corn or bell peppers, or spice it up with additional chili peppers for more heat. The combination of tender brisket and smoky BBQ flavors makes this chili a crowd-pleaser!

BBQ Bacon Wrapped Shrimp

Ingredients:

- 12 large shrimp, peeled and deveined (tails left on)
- 6 slices of bacon, cut in half crosswise
- 1/2 cup BBQ sauce (your favorite)
- Wooden toothpicks or skewers

Instructions:

1. **Prepare the Shrimp:**
   - Preheat your grill to medium-high heat, or preheat your oven to 400°F (200°C).
2. **Wrap the Shrimp:**
   - Wrap each shrimp with a half-slice of bacon, securing it with a toothpick or skewer. Make sure the bacon completely covers the shrimp.
3. **Grill or Bake the Shrimp:**
   - **Grilling Method:**
     - Place the bacon-wrapped shrimp on the preheated grill. Close the lid and grill for about 3-4 minutes per side, or until the bacon is crispy and the shrimp are pink and opaque.
   - **Oven Method:**
     - Place the bacon-wrapped shrimp on a baking sheet lined with parchment paper or aluminum foil.
     - Bake in the preheated oven for 12-15 minutes, flipping halfway through, or until the bacon is crispy and the shrimp are cooked through.
4. **Brush with BBQ Sauce:**
   - During the last few minutes of grilling or baking, brush the BBQ sauce over the bacon-wrapped shrimp. Flip them and brush the other side as well. Allow the sauce to caramelize slightly.
5. **Serve:**
   - Remove the BBQ Bacon Wrapped Shrimp from the grill or oven.
   - Serve them hot as a delicious appetizer or main dish.
6. **Enjoy:**
   - These BBQ Bacon Wrapped Shrimp are perfect for parties, game days, or any gathering where you want to impress with a savory and flavorful dish!

Feel free to adjust the amount of BBQ sauce according to your taste preferences. Serve these delicious BBQ Bacon Wrapped Shrimp with additional BBQ sauce on the side for dipping, or alongside a fresh salad or rice for a complete meal.

BBQ Pulled Pork Pizza

Ingredients:

- 1 lb pizza dough (store-bought or homemade)
- 1 cup BBQ sauce (your favorite)
- 2 cups cooked pulled pork
- 1 cup shredded mozzarella cheese
- 1/2 cup shredded cheddar cheese
- 1/4 cup thinly sliced red onion
- 1/4 cup chopped fresh cilantro
- Olive oil, for brushing
- Cornmeal or flour, for dusting

Instructions:

1. **Preheat the Oven:**
    - Preheat your oven to the highest temperature it can go (usually around 475°F to 500°F or 245°C to 260°C). If you have a pizza stone, place it in the oven while preheating.
2. **Prepare the Pizza Dough:**
    - On a lightly floured surface, roll out the pizza dough into a circle or rectangle to fit your baking sheet or pizza stone. If using a baking sheet, sprinkle it with cornmeal or flour to prevent sticking.
3. **Assemble the Pizza:**
    - Brush the rolled-out pizza dough with olive oil.
    - Spread a layer of BBQ sauce over the dough, leaving a small border around the edges for the crust.
    - Distribute the cooked pulled pork evenly over the BBQ sauce layer.
    - Sprinkle shredded mozzarella cheese and shredded cheddar cheese over the pulled pork.
    - Scatter thinly sliced red onion over the cheese.
4. **Bake the Pizza:**
    - Carefully transfer the assembled pizza to the preheated oven (on the pizza stone if using). Bake for 10-12 minutes, or until the crust is golden brown and the cheese is melted and bubbly.
5. **Finish and Serve:**
    - Remove the BBQ Pulled Pork Pizza from the oven and sprinkle chopped fresh cilantro over the top.
    - Slice the pizza and serve hot, optionally with a drizzle of extra BBQ sauce on top.
6. **Enjoy:**
    - Serve this delicious BBQ Pulled Pork Pizza as a main dish for dinner or as an appetizer for gatherings. It's packed with savory BBQ flavors and makes for a satisfying meal!

Feel free to customize this pizza by adding additional toppings such as sliced bell peppers, mushrooms, or jalapeños. The combination of tender pulled pork, tangy BBQ sauce, and gooey cheese makes this pizza a favorite for BBQ lovers!

BBQ Chicken Pizza

Ingredients:

- 1 lb pizza dough (store-bought or homemade)
- 1 cup BBQ sauce (your favorite)
- 2 cups cooked chicken breast, shredded or diced
- 1 cup shredded mozzarella cheese
- 1/2 cup shredded cheddar cheese
- 1/4 cup thinly sliced red onion
- 1/4 cup chopped fresh cilantro
- Olive oil, for brushing
- Cornmeal or flour, for dusting

Instructions:

1. **Preheat the Oven:**
    - Preheat your oven to the highest temperature it can go (usually around 475°F to 500°F or 245°C to 260°C). If you have a pizza stone, place it in the oven while preheating.
2. **Prepare the Pizza Dough:**
    - On a lightly floured surface, roll out the pizza dough into a circle or rectangle to fit your baking sheet or pizza stone. If using a baking sheet, sprinkle it with cornmeal or flour to prevent sticking.
3. **Assemble the Pizza:**
    - Brush the rolled-out pizza dough with olive oil.
    - Spread a layer of BBQ sauce over the dough, leaving a small border around the edges for the crust.
    - Distribute the cooked chicken evenly over the BBQ sauce layer.
    - Sprinkle shredded mozzarella cheese and shredded cheddar cheese over the chicken.
    - Scatter thinly sliced red onion over the cheese.
4. **Bake the Pizza:**
    - Carefully transfer the assembled pizza to the preheated oven (on the pizza stone if using). Bake for 10-12 minutes, or until the crust is golden brown and the cheese is melted and bubbly.
5. **Finish and Serve:**
    - Remove the BBQ Chicken Pizza from the oven and sprinkle chopped fresh cilantro over the top.
    - Slice the pizza and serve hot.
6. **Enjoy:**
    - Serve this delicious BBQ Chicken Pizza as a main dish for dinner or as an appetizer for gatherings. It's packed with savory BBQ flavors and makes for a satisfying meal!

Feel free to customize this pizza by adding additional toppings such as sliced bell peppers, mushrooms, or jalapeños. The combination of tender chicken, tangy BBQ sauce, and gooey cheese makes this pizza a favorite for BBQ enthusiasts!

BBQ Beef Brisket Pizza

Ingredients:

- 1 lb pizza dough (store-bought or homemade)
- 1 cup BBQ sauce (your favorite)
- 1 cup cooked beef brisket, thinly sliced or shredded
- 1 cup shredded mozzarella cheese
- 1/2 cup shredded cheddar cheese
- 1/4 cup thinly sliced red onion
- 1/4 cup chopped fresh cilantro
- Olive oil, for brushing
- Cornmeal or flour, for dusting

Instructions:

1. **Preheat the Oven:**
    - Preheat your oven to the highest temperature it can go (usually around 475°F to 500°F or 245°C to 260°C). Place a pizza stone in the oven if you have one.
2. **Prepare the Pizza Dough:**
    - On a lightly floured surface, roll out the pizza dough into a circle or rectangle to fit your baking sheet or pizza stone. Transfer the dough to a baking sheet dusted with cornmeal or flour to prevent sticking.
3. **Assemble the Pizza:**
    - Brush the rolled-out pizza dough with olive oil.
    - Spread a layer of BBQ sauce evenly over the dough, leaving a small border around the edges.
    - Distribute the cooked beef brisket slices or shredded brisket evenly over the BBQ sauce layer.
    - Sprinkle shredded mozzarella cheese and shredded cheddar cheese over the brisket.
    - Scatter thinly sliced red onion over the cheese.
4. **Bake the Pizza:**
    - Carefully transfer the assembled pizza to the preheated oven (on the pizza stone if using). Bake for 10-12 minutes, or until the crust is golden brown and the cheese is melted and bubbly.
5. **Finish and Serve:**
    - Remove the BBQ Beef Brisket Pizza from the oven and sprinkle chopped fresh cilantro over the top.
    - Slice the pizza and serve hot.
6. **Enjoy:**
    - Serve this delicious BBQ Beef Brisket Pizza as a main dish for dinner or as an appetizer for gatherings. The combination of tender brisket, tangy BBQ sauce, and melted cheese makes it a crowd-pleasing favorite!

Feel free to customize this pizza with additional toppings such as bell peppers, jalapeños, or mushrooms to suit your taste. Each bite of this BBQ Beef Brisket Pizza will be filled with savory flavors that are perfect for any occasion.

BBQ Chicken Salad

Ingredients:

- 2 boneless, skinless chicken breasts
- Salt and pepper, to taste
- 1 tablespoon olive oil
- 6 cups mixed salad greens (such as romaine, spinach, or spring mix)
- 1 cup cherry tomatoes, halved
- 1/2 cup corn kernels (fresh, canned, or thawed frozen)
- 1/2 cup black beans, drained and rinsed
- 1/4 cup red onion, thinly sliced
- 1/4 cup shredded cheddar cheese
- 1/4 cup BBQ sauce (your favorite)
- Ranch dressing or BBQ ranch dressing, for serving (optional)

Instructions:

1. **Grill the Chicken:**
   - Preheat grill or grill pan over medium-high heat.
   - Season chicken breasts with salt and pepper.
   - Drizzle olive oil over the chicken breasts.
   - Grill chicken for 6-7 minutes per side, or until fully cooked (internal temperature reaches 165°F or 74°C). Cooking time may vary depending on the thickness of the chicken breasts.
   - Remove from grill and let rest for a few minutes. Slice or chop chicken into bite-sized pieces.
2. **Prepare the Salad:**
   - In a large salad bowl, combine the mixed salad greens, cherry tomatoes, corn kernels, black beans, red onion, and shredded cheddar cheese.
3. **Assemble the Salad:**
   - Add the grilled chicken pieces to the salad bowl.
   - Drizzle BBQ sauce over the salad ingredients.
4. **Toss and Serve:**
   - Toss the salad gently to combine all ingredients and evenly coat with BBQ sauce.
   - Divide the BBQ Chicken Salad among serving plates or bowls.
5. **Optional Dressing:**
   - Serve with ranch dressing or BBQ ranch dressing on the side, if desired, for extra flavor.
6. **Enjoy:**
   - Serve immediately and enjoy this delicious BBQ Chicken Salad as a main dish. It's perfect for lunch or dinner, providing a balance of flavors and textures with the smoky BBQ chicken and crisp salad ingredients.

This BBQ Chicken Salad is versatile, and you can customize it by adding avocado, cucumbers, or your favorite salad toppings. It's a refreshing and satisfying meal that's easy to prepare and full of delicious BBQ flavor!

BBQ Pork Sandwiches

Ingredients:

- 2 lbs pork shoulder or pork butt
- Salt and pepper, to taste
- 1 cup BBQ sauce (your favorite)
- 1/2 cup chicken broth or water
- 8 sandwich buns (such as hamburger buns or brioche buns)
- Optional toppings: coleslaw, pickles, sliced onions

Instructions:

1. **Prepare the Pork:**
   - Season the pork shoulder or pork butt with salt and pepper.
   - Place the seasoned pork in a slow cooker or Instant Pot.
2. **Cook the Pork:**
   - **Slow Cooker Method:**
     - Pour the chicken broth or water around the pork.
     - Cover and cook on low for 8-10 hours or on high for 4-6 hours, until the pork is very tender and easily shreds with a fork.
   - **Instant Pot Method:**
     - Add the chicken broth or water to the Instant Pot with the pork.
     - Close the lid and set the Instant Pot to Manual/Pressure Cook mode for 60 minutes (for a 2 lb pork shoulder). Allow for natural pressure release.
3. **Shred the Pork:**
   - Once the pork is cooked and tender, remove it from the slow cooker or Instant Pot.
   - Use two forks to shred the pork into bite-sized pieces. Discard any excess fat.
4. **Add BBQ Sauce:**
   - Place the shredded pork back into the slow cooker or Instant Pot (set to sauté mode if using Instant Pot).
   - Pour the BBQ sauce over the shredded pork and mix well to coat.
5. **Assemble the Sandwiches:**
   - Toast the sandwich buns lightly, if desired.
   - Spoon the BBQ pulled pork onto the bottom half of each sandwich bun.
6. **Serve:**
   - Top the BBQ Pork Sandwiches with optional toppings such as coleslaw, pickles, or sliced onions, if desired.
   - Place the top half of the sandwich bun on top.
7. **Enjoy:**
   - Serve these delicious BBQ Pork Sandwiches immediately. They are perfect for lunch, dinner, or any casual gathering. The tender and flavorful pulled pork combined with the tangy BBQ sauce makes for a satisfying and comforting meal!

This recipe is versatile, and you can adjust the seasonings and BBQ sauce according to your taste preferences. Serve these sandwiches with a side of potato chips, fries, or a fresh green salad for a complete meal.

BBQ Beef Sandwiches

Ingredients:

- 2 lbs beef chuck roast or brisket
- Salt and pepper, to taste
- 1 cup BBQ sauce (your favorite)
- 1/2 cup beef broth or water
- 8 sandwich buns (such as hamburger buns or brioche buns)
- Optional toppings: sliced pickles, coleslaw, sliced onions

Instructions:

1. **Prepare the Beef:**
    - Season the beef chuck roast or brisket with salt and pepper.
2. **Cook the Beef:**
    - **Slow Cooker Method:**
        - Place the seasoned beef in a slow cooker.
        - Pour the beef broth or water around the beef.
        - Cover and cook on low for 8-10 hours or on high for 4-6 hours, until the beef is very tender and easily shreds with a fork.
    - **Instant Pot Method:**
        - Add the beef broth or water to the Instant Pot with the seasoned beef.
        - Close the lid and set the Instant Pot to Manual/Pressure Cook mode for 60 minutes (for a 2 lb beef chuck roast). Allow for natural pressure release.
3. **Shred the Beef:**
    - Once the beef is cooked and tender, remove it from the slow cooker or Instant Pot.
    - Use two forks to shred the beef into bite-sized pieces. Discard any excess fat.
4. **Add BBQ Sauce:**
    - Place the shredded beef back into the slow cooker or Instant Pot (set to sauté mode if using Instant Pot).
    - Pour the BBQ sauce over the shredded beef and mix well to coat.
5. **Assemble the Sandwiches:**
    - Toast the sandwich buns lightly, if desired.
    - Spoon the BBQ shredded beef onto the bottom half of each sandwich bun.
6. **Serve:**
    - Top the BBQ Beef Sandwiches with optional toppings such as sliced pickles, coleslaw, or sliced onions, if desired.
    - Place the top half of the sandwich bun on top.
7. **Enjoy:**

- Serve these delicious BBQ Beef Sandwiches immediately. They are perfect for lunch, dinner, or any casual gathering. The tender and flavorful shredded beef combined with the tangy BBQ sauce makes for a hearty and satisfying meal!

Feel free to adjust the seasonings and BBQ sauce according to your taste preferences. Serve these sandwiches with a side of potato chips, fries, or a fresh green salad for a complete and delicious meal.

BBQ Beef Ribs

Ingredients:

- 3-4 lbs beef ribs (short ribs or beef back ribs)
- Salt and pepper, to taste
- 1 cup BBQ sauce (your favorite)
- 1/2 cup beef broth or water
- Optional: dry rub seasoning (paprika, garlic powder, onion powder, cayenne pepper)

Instructions:

1. **Prepare the Ribs:**
   - If using beef back ribs, remove the membrane from the back of the ribs for better seasoning penetration.
2. **Season the Ribs:**
   - Season the beef ribs generously with salt and pepper. Optionally, you can rub them with a dry rub seasoning mix for additional flavor. Let them sit at room temperature for about 30 minutes before cooking.
3. **Preheat the Grill or Oven:**
   - **Grill Method:**
     - Preheat your grill to medium heat (around 300-325°F or 150-160°C). Set up for indirect cooking.
   - **Oven Method:**
     - Preheat your oven to 300°F (150°C). Place a rack in the middle of the oven.
4. **Cook the Ribs:**
   - **Grill Method:**
     - Place the seasoned beef ribs on the grill over indirect heat.
     - Close the lid and cook for 2-3 hours, turning occasionally, until the ribs are tender. Brush with BBQ sauce during the last 30 minutes of cooking.
   - **Oven Method:**
     - Place the seasoned beef ribs on a baking sheet lined with aluminum foil or parchment paper.
     - Pour beef broth or water into the baking sheet to create steam.
     - Cover the ribs tightly with aluminum foil and bake for 2-2.5 hours, until the meat is tender and easily pulls away from the bone.
     - Remove the foil, brush the ribs with BBQ sauce, and return to the oven for another 15-20 minutes, allowing the sauce to caramelize.
5. **Rest and Serve:**
   - Remove the BBQ Beef Ribs from the grill or oven and let them rest for a few minutes before serving.
   - Optionally, brush with more BBQ sauce before serving.
6. **Enjoy:**

- Serve these delicious BBQ Beef Ribs with your favorite sides like coleslaw, baked beans, or cornbread for a complete meal. They are perfect for gatherings or a satisfying family dinner!

This recipe can be adjusted based on your preferred BBQ sauce and seasoning choices. The slow cooking process ensures that the beef ribs are tender and infused with smoky BBQ flavors, making them a favorite for BBQ enthusiasts!

BBQ Brisket Tacos

Ingredients:

- 1 lb beef brisket
- Salt and pepper, to taste
- 1 cup BBQ sauce (your favorite)
- 1/2 cup beef broth or water
- 8-10 small flour or corn tortillas
- Optional toppings: shredded lettuce, diced tomatoes, sliced avocado, chopped cilantro, lime wedges

Instructions:

1. **Prepare the Brisket:**
    - Season the beef brisket with salt and pepper on all sides.
2. **Cook the Brisket:**
    - Preheat your oven to 300°F (150°C).
    - Place the seasoned brisket in a roasting pan or baking dish.
    - Pour beef broth or water into the pan.
    - Cover tightly with aluminum foil and roast for 4-5 hours, or until the brisket is tender and easily shreds with a fork.
3. **Shred and BBQ Sauce:**
    - Remove the brisket from the oven and shred it using two forks.
    - Transfer the shredded brisket to a bowl and mix with BBQ sauce until well coated.
4. **Warm Tortillas:**
    - Heat the tortillas on a skillet over medium heat until warm and slightly charred, about 1-2 minutes per side. Alternatively, warm them in the microwave wrapped in a damp paper towel.
5. **Assemble the Tacos:**
    - Spoon the BBQ brisket into the warmed tortillas.
    - Add optional toppings such as shredded lettuce, diced tomatoes, sliced avocado, chopped cilantro, and a squeeze of lime juice.
6. **Serve:**
    - Serve the BBQ Brisket Tacos immediately.
    - Enjoy these delicious tacos as a main dish for lunch or dinner. They are perfect for gatherings or family meals!

This recipe is versatile, and you can adjust the toppings and BBQ sauce according to your preference. These BBQ Brisket Tacos are sure to be a hit with their tender brisket and bold flavors wrapped in a warm tortilla!

BBQ Pork Belly

Ingredients:

- 2 lbs pork belly, skin removed
- Salt and pepper, to taste
- 1 cup BBQ sauce (your favorite)
- 1/2 cup apple cider vinegar
- 1/4 cup soy sauce
- 1/4 cup brown sugar
- 2 cloves garlic, minced
- 1 teaspoon smoked paprika
- 1/2 teaspoon cayenne pepper (optional, for heat)
- Vegetable oil, for grilling

Instructions:

1. **Prepare the Pork Belly:**
   - Pat dry the pork belly with paper towels. Score the fat side of the pork belly with a sharp knife in a crosshatch pattern, being careful not to cut into the meat.
2. **Marinate the Pork Belly:**
   - In a bowl, mix together BBQ sauce, apple cider vinegar, soy sauce, brown sugar, minced garlic, smoked paprika, and cayenne pepper (if using).
   - Place the pork belly in a large resealable plastic bag or shallow dish. Pour half of the marinade over the pork belly, making sure it is well coated. Reserve the other half of the marinade for basting.
3. **Marinate Overnight (Optional):**
   - For deeper flavor, refrigerate the pork belly in the marinade for at least 2 hours or overnight.
4. **Preheat the Grill:**
   - Preheat your grill to medium-high heat (about 375-400°F or 190-200°C). Brush the grill grates with vegetable oil to prevent sticking.
5. **Grill the Pork Belly:**
   - Remove the pork belly from the marinade and discard the marinade.
   - Place the pork belly on the grill, fat side down first, and cook for 5-7 minutes per side, or until nicely charred and caramelized.
   - Lower the heat to medium-low or move the pork belly to a cooler part of the grill to prevent burning. Close the lid and continue grilling for another 20-30 minutes, basting occasionally with the reserved marinade, until the internal temperature reaches 190°F (88°C) and the meat is tender.
6. **Rest and Slice:**
   - Remove the BBQ Pork Belly from the grill and let it rest for 10 minutes before slicing.
   - Slice the pork belly into thick slices or cubes.

7. **Serve:**
    - Serve the BBQ Pork Belly slices or cubes hot, with additional BBQ sauce on the side if desired.
    - Enjoy this flavorful and succulent BBQ Pork Belly as a main dish, paired with sides like coleslaw, roasted vegetables, or cornbread.

This BBQ Pork Belly recipe offers a perfect balance of smoky, sweet, and savory flavors, making it a delightful choice for BBQ enthusiasts and special occasions. Adjust the marinade ingredients and grilling time based on your preferences and grill setup.

BBQ Chicken Thighs

Ingredients:

- 8 bone-in, skin-on chicken thighs
- Salt and pepper, to taste
- 1 cup BBQ sauce (your favorite)
- Optional: olive oil or vegetable oil for grilling

Instructions:

1. **Prepare the Chicken Thighs:**
   - Pat dry the chicken thighs with paper towels.
   - Season both sides of the chicken thighs generously with salt and pepper.
2. **Preheat the Grill (or Oven):**
   - **Grill Method:**
     - Preheat your grill to medium-high heat (about 375-400°F or 190-200°C).
     - Brush the grill grates with oil to prevent sticking.
   - **Oven Method:**
     - Preheat your oven to 400°F (200°C).
     - Line a baking sheet with aluminum foil or parchment paper.
3. **Grill (or Bake) the Chicken Thighs:**
   - **Grill Method:**
     - Place the seasoned chicken thighs on the grill, skin side down first.
     - Grill for 6-7 minutes per side, or until the skin is crispy and golden brown.
     - Brush the top side of the chicken thighs with BBQ sauce during the last 2-3 minutes of cooking. Flip and brush the other side with BBQ sauce as well.
     - Continue grilling until the internal temperature of the chicken thighs reaches 165°F (75°C) and they are cooked through.
   - **Oven Method:**
     - Arrange the seasoned chicken thighs on the prepared baking sheet, skin side up.
     - Bake in the preheated oven for 25-30 minutes.
     - Brush the chicken thighs with BBQ sauce halfway through baking, and again in the last 5 minutes of baking.
4. **Serve:**
   - Remove the BBQ Chicken Thighs from the grill or oven.
   - Let them rest for a few minutes before serving.
   - Serve hot, garnished with chopped parsley or green onions if desired.
5. **Enjoy:**
   - BBQ Chicken Thighs are perfect for serving with your favorite sides such as coleslaw, cornbread, or grilled vegetables. They make a delicious main dish for any occasion!

This recipe is easy to customize with different BBQ sauce flavors or additional seasonings. Whether you grill or bake them, BBQ Chicken Thighs are sure to be a crowd-pleaser with their juicy and flavorful meat paired with crispy skin.

BBQ Beef Burgers

Ingredients:

- 1 lb ground beef (preferably 80% lean)
- Salt and pepper, to taste
- 1/4 cup BBQ sauce (your favorite)
- 4 hamburger buns
- Optional toppings: lettuce, tomato slices, red onion slices, cheese slices (cheddar or pepper jack), pickles

Instructions:

1. **Prepare the Burger Patties:**
    - In a mixing bowl, combine the ground beef, salt, pepper, and BBQ sauce. Mix gently until well combined.
2. **Form the Patties:**
    - Divide the beef mixture into 4 equal portions.
    - Shape each portion into a round patty, about 1/2 to 3/4 inch thick. Press a slight indentation in the center of each patty to prevent them from puffing up while cooking.
3. **Preheat the Grill (or Pan):**
    - **Grill Method:**
        - Preheat your grill to medium-high heat.
        - Brush the grill grates with oil to prevent sticking.
    - **Stovetop Method:**
        - Heat a grill pan or large skillet over medium-high heat. Add a drizzle of oil to coat the pan.
4. **Cook the Burgers:**
    - **Grill Method:**
        - Place the burger patties on the preheated grill.
        - Grill for 4-5 minutes per side, or until the burgers reach your desired level of doneness (160°F or 71°C for medium).
        - Brush the top side of each burger patty with additional BBQ sauce during the last 1-2 minutes of cooking.
    - **Stovetop Method:**
        - Place the burger patties in the hot skillet or grill pan.
        - Cook for 4-5 minutes per side, flipping once, until the burgers are cooked through.
5. **Toast the Burger Buns:**
    - During the last minute of cooking, place the hamburger buns, cut side down, on the grill or in the skillet to lightly toast.
6. **Assemble the Burgers:**

- Place each BBQ Beef Burger patty on the bottom half of a toasted hamburger bun.
- Add your desired toppings such as lettuce, tomato slices, red onion slices, cheese slices, and pickles.

7. **Serve:**
   - Serve the BBQ Beef Burgers immediately, with additional BBQ sauce on the side if desired.
   - Enjoy these delicious burgers as a main dish, paired with fries, potato salad, or a fresh green salad.

This BBQ Beef Burger recipe is versatile, and you can adjust the seasoning and toppings according to your taste preferences. It's a perfect choice for a summer barbecue or casual dinner, offering a tasty twist on the classic burger experience!

BBQ Smoked Chicken

Ingredients:

- 4-6 chicken pieces (such as drumsticks, thighs, or breasts), skin-on
- Salt and pepper, to taste
- BBQ rub or seasoning (optional)
- 1 cup BBQ sauce (your favorite)
- Wood chips or chunks for smoking (hickory, mesquite, applewood, etc.)
- Olive oil or vegetable oil, for brushing

Instructions:

1. **Prepare the Chicken:**
   - Rinse the chicken pieces under cold water and pat them dry with paper towels.
   - Season the chicken pieces generously with salt and pepper. Optionally, rub them with BBQ rub or seasoning for additional flavor.
2. **Prepare the Smoker:**
   - If using a charcoal smoker, light the charcoal and let it burn until the coals are ashed over. Add soaked wood chips or chunks to the coals.
   - If using an electric or gas smoker, preheat it according to the manufacturer's instructions and add wood chips or chunks to the smoker box.
3. **Smoke the Chicken:**
   - Brush the chicken pieces lightly with olive oil or vegetable oil to help the seasoning stick.
   - Place the chicken pieces on the smoker racks, ensuring they are not touching each other for even smoking.
   - Close the smoker lid and smoke the chicken at a temperature of around 225-250°F (107-121°C) for 2-3 hours, depending on the size of the chicken pieces. Add more wood chips or chunks as needed to maintain smoke.
4. **Glaze with BBQ Sauce:**
   - About 30 minutes before the chicken is done smoking, brush each piece with BBQ sauce, using a basting brush.
   - Continue smoking until the internal temperature of the chicken reaches 165°F (74°C) and the juices run clear when pierced with a knife.
5. **Rest and Serve:**
   - Remove the BBQ Smoked Chicken from the smoker and let it rest for 5-10 minutes before serving.
   - Serve hot, garnished with chopped parsley or green onions if desired.
6. **Enjoy:**
   - BBQ Smoked Chicken is perfect for serving with your favorite sides such as cornbread, coleslaw, or baked beans. It makes for a delicious main dish for any barbecue or outdoor gathering!

This recipe allows you to enjoy tender and flavorful BBQ Smoked Chicken with a delightful smoky aroma that enhances its natural juiciness. Adjust the smoking time and BBQ sauce application based on your smoker type and personal taste preferences.

BBQ Pulled Pork Egg Rolls

Ingredients:

- 1 cup BBQ pulled pork (homemade or store-bought)
- 8 egg roll wrappers
- 1 cup coleslaw mix (shredded cabbage and carrots)
- 1/4 cup BBQ sauce (plus extra for serving)
- Vegetable oil, for frying
- Optional: sliced green onions for garnish

Instructions:

1. **Prepare the BBQ Pulled Pork:**
   - If using store-bought BBQ pulled pork, heat it according to package instructions. If making homemade pulled pork, ensure it's fully cooked and shredded.
2. **Assemble the Egg Rolls:**
   - Lay an egg roll wrapper on a clean surface with one corner pointing towards you (diamond shape).
   - Place a spoonful of BBQ pulled pork in the center of the wrapper.
   - Top the pulled pork with a spoonful of coleslaw mix.
   - Drizzle about a teaspoon of BBQ sauce over the coleslaw mix.
3. **Roll the Egg Rolls:**
   - Fold the bottom corner of the wrapper over the filling.
   - Fold the sides of the wrapper towards the center.
   - Roll tightly towards the top corner to seal the egg roll. Use a dab of water to seal the edges if needed.
4. **Fry the Egg Rolls:**
   - Heat vegetable oil in a deep skillet or pot to 350°F (175°C).
   - Carefully place the egg rolls seam-side down in the hot oil, a few at a time, without overcrowding the pan.
   - Fry for 3-4 minutes, turning occasionally, until golden brown and crispy.
   - Remove the egg rolls with a slotted spoon and place them on a plate lined with paper towels to drain excess oil.
5. **Serve:**
   - Serve the BBQ Pulled Pork Egg Rolls hot, with extra BBQ sauce for dipping.
   - Optionally, garnish with sliced green onions for added freshness.
6. **Enjoy:**
   - These BBQ Pulled Pork Egg Rolls are perfect as appetizers, snacks, or as a main dish with a side salad. The combination of tender pulled pork, crunchy coleslaw, and crispy egg roll wrapper makes them a crowd-pleasing favorite!

Feel free to adjust the filling quantities and BBQ sauce to suit your taste preferences. These egg rolls are best served fresh and hot, straight from the frying pan for maximum crispiness and flavor.

Printed in the USA
CPSIA information can be obtained
at www.ICGtesting.com
CBHW081709300724
12432CB00022B/479